Advance Praise for

"*Angels in the OR* is about a spiritual journey of a very alive and honest woman. She hides nothing from her truthful account of living dying and living more fully. Tricia Barker is an engaging and compassionate person who has found her purpose in life. Following her beautifully written story will confirm the readers about their own journey. Share the light with her as she brings the love into our world."

—Howard Storm, author
of *My Descent into Death*, is a
minister, writer, and painter

"This is one book you won't want to miss! *Angels in the OR: What Dying Taught Me about Healing, Survival, and Transformation* is exceptionally beautiful and enthralling. Tricia Barker's near-death experience is remarkable. With each turn of the page there are **powerful insights and understandings that could change your life.** This outstanding book is expertly written, remarkably easy to read, and enthusiastically recommended."

—Jeffrey Long, M.D., author
of *New York Times* bestselling
Evidence of the Afterlife: The Science of Near-Death Experiences

"Tricia Barker's *Angels in the OR* is far more than the story of a profound near-death experience. It is a book of profound spiritual wisdom, which comes from the author's life of healing from great physical pain, emotional trauma, and most of all from her inspiring dedication to her life as a teacher. I was deeply moved by this book. The light and infinite love of God often shines through Tricia Barker's words."

—Kenneth Ring, Ph.D.,
retired Professor Emeritus of
psychology at the University of
Connecticut and a researcher within
the field of near-death studies

What Dying Taught Me About Healing, Survival, and Transformation

ANGELS IN THE OR

TRICIA BARKER

A POST HILL PRESS BOOK

ISBN: 978-1-64293-159-4
ISBN (eBook): 978-1-64293-160-0

Angels in the OR:
What Dying Taught Me About Healing,
Survival, and Transformation

Cover art by Tricia Principe, principedesign.com
Author Photo by Jazmin Marin

All people, locations, events, and situations are portrayed to the best of the author's memory. While all of the events described are true, many names and identifying details have been changed to protect the privacy of the people involved.

Post Hill Press, LLC
New York • Nashville
posthillpress.com

Published in the United States of America

CONTENTS

FOREWORD

The light shines in the darkness, and the darkness has not overcome it.
—John 1:5

Those who have had near-death experiences open a window to what exists after death for those of us who have not yet had a glimpse of it. The sill widens to allow us new insight and an infusion of light.

One of the remarkable things I have learned through my research of near-death experiences and those in coma is that often the most compromised of physical bodies have the most transcendental experiences.

Imagine your back completely crushed in a car crash, so forcefully that you are constrained by a body cast for months. Tricia Barker shares with us how, in moments after an accident, she was touched by a profound radiance. Its presence imbues her storytelling and her life.

> *The two angels sent waves of intense light, which transferred many messages to me all at once. The light emitted from the eyes of the angels flowed directly into my spirit*

> *body, allowing me to access information faster than the fastest possible broadband speed. Messages were given in the form of completed thoughts and feelings, not individual words. The knowledge they sent into my spirit form not only felt comforting, but it also altered the way I viewed everything about my life.*

Light is central to the accounts of people who have had near-death experiences, so much so that books about the topic often include the word in the title: *Transformed by the Light, Lessons from the Light, Divine Light,* and *The Light Beyond*. Tricia describes her experience of the light:

> *Light seemed to contain both healing power and knowledge… A large part of me never wanted to leave the safety of that place. I felt no stress and more love than I ever imagined possible. I felt more joy and contentment than even the brightest moments this life ever provided, and I did not want to return to my body. No person had ever shown me a love like this love. I had no idea it was possible to feel this good. If a soul could smile, then my soul smiled, and I drowsed comfortably without worry.*

In every way, this book is about following the light and trusting it even when everything around us is aimed at extinguishing it. Some books about NDEs have a kind of fairytale ending, as they share the miracles that lead to grand transformations. However, Tricia offers a more sober, measured view of the near-death experience and how life unfolds in its wake. The book is a reminder for me that monumental change occurs very often in small steps. Even after the greatest revelations, life may bring us setbacks, intensified self-doubt, challenges to our new-found wisdom. The divine, Tricia reminds us, is ever-present, but so are the challenges of our very ordinary lives, as we reconcile past trespasses with the present and seek love, meaning, and self-confidence.

As Tricia shares her life story with us—as she rises from poverty, heals from a devastating car accident, and the collisions that love can bring—she also shares the light, the powerful but gentle, ever-present light that inspired her to become a teacher, and find new ways to love and live.

> *One of the most important things I have learned from dying is that death is not real but feels like birth into a new realm of understanding. We go on, and we keep learning and exploring. We continue to understand our connection to God and how deeply we are loved.*

Once Tricia has fought back to health from her immobilizing car accident, she is only in her mid-twenties, and travels in hope to fully heed the words of wisdom of her angels to "become a teacher." She lands in South Korea to teach English, but while living in this country she is brutally raped. And yet, the light persists. The light guides her through this moment so that she can later help students who survived similar traumas.

In Tricia's story, I see my story, and I imagine you will see yours as well because it is a tale of how we must struggle sometimes to bring the light of our spirits into a world that can be cruel. Tricia captivated me; her writing is so beautifully detailed and authentic as she shares not only the breathtaking moments of near-death but also the very challenges of bringing the light back, as she confronts the realities of violence against children and women, unsympathetic institutions, and the classrooms of students who bring lifetimes of rage and frustration with them.

I recognize in her story the incalculable distance at times between the sacred and the profane. How many of us have had deeply spiritual moments perhaps in meditation, at our houses of worship, or simply walking on the beach, or on a mountain trail at sunrise? In those moments, we may feel profound connection to Source, and its palpable presence in our lives until we are back at work or betrayed by a sweetheart or assaulted unexpectedly.

What makes *Angels in the OR* so compelling to me is that not only does it ride the remarkable wave of Tricia Barker's near-death experience, but that it is also pulled by the currents of history as she questions how we can best live a good life and bring the light into the shadows of this world.

The questions Tricia asks, and the answers she shares with us, speak to the issues of our time, as the #metoo movement and human trafficking gain greater attention and more people are asking questions about what it means to be a woman or a man in these turbulent times. And how can we all balance the realities of our sexual identities with what Tricia describes as our eternal self?

> *I couldn't find an answer to why women were often treated as objects both in the U.S. and in Asia. I knew that I was an eternal being, far greater and vaster than my physical form, but being in the body of a young woman was beginning to make my*

> *journey feel treacherous… How was I going to help other women? My gender seemed an unfair cross to bear, and I missed what it felt like to shed my gender and be a spirit.*

We all stand in both worlds with the constraints of our bodies and the limitless, timelessness of our souls and spirits. I loved that Tricia put a voice to this reality and throughout the book, she teaches us of the polarities of our lives as we swing between our embodied identities as men and women and that of being eternal souls; our ability to betray one another and our great capacity of love; the light-filled innocence of our spirits and the darker forces of those who bring suffering to others.

> *The truth is, I would've preferred to stay on the other side, but I didn't have a choice. The decision was made for me to return. I felt my soul sucked backwards through a dark wind toward my body. Re-entering my physical body felt like being swallowed by a painful, narrowing darkness.*

Many of us who have not had NDEs can also relate to the *painful, narrowing darkness* Tricia describes. How do we bring our spiritual practices and the expansion of spirit we may feel when we engage in them into our day-to-day lives? We hear from certain spiritual perspectives that we each individually create and manifest our own reality, and yet, how do we make sense of this in a world where there are real injustices? Tricia writes:

> *Guilt wouldn't help me heal, and the only thing that seemed accurate is that*

> *rape happens to young women all over the world and the statistics are horrifying. My vibration didn't manifest a stalker or this rape; rather, the collective unconscious had created rape culture—a culture that gives men power over women and doesn't often hold them responsible for violence against women. From that point forward, my power would lie in my ability to survive PTSD, to learn ways to heal, and to fight to create a safer world.*

Part of Tricia's answer lies in first learning to fully love ourselves as we also turn that light outward: *We are intrinsically and deeply connected to this powerful divine light, and it is our divine right to love ourselves the way God loves us.*

The answer also rests in our acknowledging the very real injustices that exist and, in whatever ways we can, bring light to them.

When Tricia Barker died, the light of God instructed her to return to her life and pursue a career as a teacher. Teaching, at its best, reveals the inherent goodness of both teacher and student. Teaching also heals, as it levels the field so that all can have the tools to express their voices and find mastery in the world.

> *I walked with one of them into town and told him that teaching was a holy profession to me. Though I might make mistakes in the rest of my life, I wanted to be there for their soul's journey in any small way.*

The light offered Tricia a remarkable gift as she was called to teach. True callings have that quality of the angels or muses sitting on our shoulders, whispering in our ears as they guide our way, often as we mend what is shattered:

> *I could read the emotions of students, knowing when they zoned out, when ideas and connections happened in their brains, and when their hearts were moved. I could tell when they squinted in disbelief, so I pushed harder, breaking through their cognitive barriers. I felt the presence of my angels at times, taking over my body and giving me the right words at the right time.*

Tricia extends the light of her near-death experience to the neglected voices and perspectives of her students and the institutions where she works. For thirty years, I also taught in some of the most under-served neighborhoods. I have witnessed the power of teaching and writing to shed light on students' truths and empower their lives. As Tricia explains:

> *I made him promise to keep writing about his life and to write his way out of that life. I did my best to give him a thread of light to guide him to a new place in life. For a few magical moments, I watched his face transform as he looked at me, believing that I saw something special in him.*

When we see our learners with the very eyes that the angels see us, we can inspire them to greater good, just as our angels inspire us. Tricia followed the guidance of her NDE and has brought the gift of learning to her students. Now she also delivers lessons to those of us whose classrooms have no walls.

Angels in OR offers true inspiration and affirmation that something beyond this Earth exists and can be accessed for personal and social good. This book also invites each of us to consider the realities of our broken world and our broken selves and how in the very fissures we may find healing and light.

Lisa Smartt
Author of *Words at the Threshold*
Athens, Georgia 2018

PART I

CHAPTER ONE

THE ACCIDENT

"It is worth dying to find out what life is."
—T.S. Eliot

I am one of the worst passengers you could ever have in your car. I hang on to the door, bite my nails, and narrate everything happening on the highway—just in case the driver didn't immediately see the red taillights of the car five thousand feet away. I wouldn't want myself as a passenger, but I don't enjoy driving either.

The only time I'm not afraid in a car is when I'm driving over tall bridges. I imagine if the car were to somehow veer off and fall, the impact would result in instant death. You see, I'm not afraid of death. I *am* afraid of the physical pain from surviving a car wreck. I've survived one before, on a Sunday morning in April 1994. That was when my 1988 Honda Civic Hatchback collided with a SUV at sixty-five miles per hour.

I was twenty-two years old and in my best physical shape since starting college. I had been training hard for the Austin

Capitol 10K, even allowing myself to dream of placing or winning; however unlikely, the image of success made me run faster.

I had a lot of pain to outrun, especially some harsh words from a man I'd loved more deeply than I believed I could love. I pictured outrunning the image of his beautiful face marked by his cruel mouth and devilish goatee. I ran away from his prediction that terrible things would happen in my life and he didn't want to be around to see any of them happen.

I always practiced the last mile at full speed, grimace-smiling as I reached speeds that were damned fast, nearing my five-minute mile goal. I ran toward graduation, only a few short weeks away. I ran through the pain toward a bright sunlight that represented my future in my mind's eye. I had no idea on the day of the race that my decision not to stop for coffee at 7-Eleven, as was my habit, would alter my life forever.

The wreck seemed to happen instantly. I barely even had time to move my foot to the brake before the impact of the collision. A tall, broad-shouldered man—I would later learn his name was Mister Flores—got out of his SUV holding his two-year old daughter, blood streaming down his face. His windshield had shattered and embedded pieces of glass in his forehead and head; my heart pounded furiously when I realized his little girl was injured as well. A tiny stream of blood ran from her hairline down her face.

As gruesome as Mister Flores and his tiny daughter looked, I quickly realized I was in much worse shape because I couldn't get out of the car. I couldn't even reach my registration and insurance in the glove box, and my body felt incredibly hot. I sat slumped against the driver's door, screaming loudly out the window, "I'm sorry! I'm so sorry! I'm sorry!"

I didn't know if the accident was my fault, but I assumed it might have been and felt relieved that this hadn't happened coming back from a party or a night out on Sixth Street. I know the first light at the long, curved intersection at Guadalupe and Lamar was yellow. I know I gunned it, hoping to get a good parking spot for the race. I know I wasn't aware of anything until it was too late, and his vehicle was barreling toward mine rapidly, yet as if we were in slow motion those last few seconds. My car crumpled up around me like a soda can, and the small bones in my right ankle crunched immediately. Running the Capitol 10K was clearly not happening that day.

Mister Flores refused to look at me and concentrated on getting someone to stop for us by waving his right arm around while holding his daughter to him with his left arm. I remember the silence in my car once I stopped screaming out apologies. I looked down at my fractured ankle and bleeding knees and thought, perhaps melodramatically as twenty-two-year-olds are prone to do, that my broken outside now mirrored my broken inside.

I could barely stand the silence inside my car as I realized my fate was out of my hands and rested instead on who might decide to stop for us. Three cars drove by as Mister Flores tried to wave them down. A group of teenagers slammed on their brakes, screamed in horror, and sped off.

Eventually, a good Samaritan, who happened to be a nurse, stopped and sat in the car with me while her boyfriend drove to a gas station to call for an ambulance. I barely remember her—just her soft, comforting voice and long, auburn hair.

She told me that the paramedics would put me on a board, but she didn't tell me how much it would hurt to lie on that board, looking up at the puffy cumulus clouds and wishing I was at the race. I had no option but to give over control in that moment, and I briefly beseeched God in my terror. I hadn't prayed since childhood, and I had no idea if my words would matter. Still, I imagined my small plea flying across the sky, like a random bird I caught sight of before the ambulance door slammed shut.

On the slow ride to the hospital, I ran through possibilities in my mind: would I walk or be in a wheelchair, live with chronic pain or run again, have a long recovery or die in surgery? At the time of my accident I considered myself agnostic, believing with some fear and sadness that we simply cease to exist when we die. Though I was raised Christian, I didn't care for the hypocrisy and judgment I had observed in churches.

I worshipped intelligence, and I didn't hear eloquence, good rational appeals, evidence-based reasoning, or much of anything that appealed to me at church. Having grown up poor, I always placed last in the fashion show in our place of worship, so I worshiped in lecture halls. I made friends at parties and bars, laughing and dancing late into the night.

The ambulance seemed to be moving at five miles per hour; I was anxious for answers about my condition, but I would do a lot more waiting before being told the full extent of my injuries. When Mister Flores, his daughter, and I arrived at the ER, attendants quickly took us each in separate directions.

I met Missus Flores, the mother of the man in the other vehicle. She sat with me and prayed for me, assuring me that her son and granddaughter would be fine. They were both immediately taken into plastic surgery for the cuts on their foreheads. The liability insurance I had on my car assured their care. Missus Flores's kindness and willingness to stay with me touched me, and I was relieved to hear that her family members had suffered no broken bones or internal injuries. The image of the little girl intermittently crying and clinging to her dad's shirt haunted me all morning.

I tried to be a kind, albeit somewhat weepy patient for the first eight hours, asking many questions about spinal injuries and possible outcomes. The nurses refused to speculate but also assured me that people do walk again after fracturing their backs. My grandmother showed up first and thanked Missus Flores for waiting with me. Other family members arrived and then went away to eat, talk with each other, and find hotel rooms.

As hours rolled by, I was often left unattended in the hallway outside the room where the MRI and X-rays were taken. This isolation stoked my fears, and I began to lose my senses. The florescent lights beating down on my broken body were horrifying, and the snippets of conversation I overheard from nurses were discouraging. I knew three vertebrae in my mid-back were fractured, but I wasn't allowed even Tylenol because I would have to go in for surgery as soon as possible. The pain was hot, intense, and unbearable, but the nurses ignored my pleas for relief, briefly explaining that the surgeon had to make the call about palliative care in case I had extensive internal injuries. With hindsight, I realize the medical necessity of not quashing my pain in the moment.

Eight hours after the accident, I overheard a nurse, standing behind a curtain, place the phone back on the wall and say, "I called him, but he's not coming in. He's staying on the golf course because she doesn't have health insurance."

The other nurse replied, "Typical. What are we gonna do with her?"

The nurse's frustration slammed into me with palpable force. I felt vulnerable and extra sensitive lying on that cold metal plate. The surgeon's disregard for me sent me over the edge, and after so many hours in agonizing pain, I lost my composure. Through an imagined tunnel in time, I imagined him clearly—preppy clothes, a polo with a contrasting color on the collar, white baseball cap, short gray hair, jocular, full of himself, cold, and not that great of a golfer, just decent after a lot of practice.

I hoped his arteries clogged up from the French fries he surely ate at lunch. I hoped his future heart attack had complications. I hoped he survived that heart attack only to have a crazed man with a tire tool randomly beat him senseless one morning just after he grabbed a cup of coffee. I hoped the coffee spilled on him. I hoped he cried hot tears for his broken body, strapped to a board as if he were an animal waiting for an experiment to begin and his life to end. I hoped he felt like me. No painkillers, just the knowledge that his back was broken, and the neurosurgeon was *choosing* not to be available.

Of course, I didn't know that surgeon personally, but I guessed at his type: a man who maybe faced a few obstacles in adolescence but made his way in the world and thought to hell with everyone else trying to scramble toward a better life. And I was trying. My parents refused to let me consider expensive university options, but my senior year I applied for scholarships like a woman obsessed and received several.

I was proud to get into The University of Texas at Austin, and admittance gave me the opportunity to blend in with wealthier, more privileged kids. I took out student loans and opened credit cards to purchase Nikes, workout clothes, Doc Martens, and alternative wear for parties. I felt visible for the first time in my life, even desirable.

Growing up, I never had braces, yearly checkups, or health insurance. It never crossed my mind to purchase any. I assumed I would get health insurance with my first job out of college. Did the surgeon bother to ask how old I was, if I was a student, or anything about me? Probably not. He probably only asked, "Does she have insurance?"

I'm sure I'd served him or his type drinks at the bars I worked at in Austin, navigating my way through crowds of people and wearing boots and miniskirts or short, leather shorts to display my body for better tips. Now, my body was just a body again, something that wouldn't impact his income positively. I never realized how difficult it was to scramble up the social ladder until that moment. I never realized that my life was a throwaway to some people. Beneath the surface, I had a stockpile of rage, and when I heard that surgeon's response, the dam broke and it all came flowing out.

I yelled at the nurses, at no one, at everyone, and mostly at the large, white rectangles on the ceiling, "Fuck him, fuck him, fuck that surgeon! I'm a college student. Not a loser. I will not be dismissed. I need this operation so I can walk! Fuck him, fuck him, fuck him!"

My mom, aunts, and grandmother exited the room, terrified at my outbursts. I imagine I wailed about the surgeon for a while, but my cursing eventually became moaning which transitioned into loud sobbing, full of self-pity and misery.

After I eventually lost my voice, quiet tears flowed down each side of my face for hours. By nightfall, my left leg had lost most of its feeling, and I had lost hope, simply watching time pass by.

When Doctor Flawn, a young, blonde surgeon looked at my chart and told me she was an off-duty neurosurgeon, I came alive. I grabbed her arm and said what I couldn't say to the man on the golf course: "Please operate on me. I'm sorry I don't have insurance. I'm a student, and I swear I'll kill myself if I can't walk again."

She nodded, made eye contact with me, and then studied my chart silently.

For a magical split second, Doctor Flawn saw me as a human being, and I knew this meant she would help me. I felt fortunate that we resembled each other a little physically and hoped this might make her connect with me. She was probably fifteen years older than I was, a little younger than my mom.

I felt thrilled to meet a successful woman because I hadn't met many growing up in a small town in East Texas. Women who were my professors at U.T. were the only other successful women I had encountered. I knew my grandmother would be astonished that a woman would be my neurosurgeon, but I felt thrilled.

For the first time in twelve hours, I behaved like a persuasive, rational human being; I asked her questions about where she lived in Austin and where she had studied medicine. I gave our brief interaction my charming all. I expressed concern for her well-being when she informed me that she had been on duty for forty-four hours and that she must go home, eat, and get a bit of rest before operating on me. I truly believed Doctor Flawn would return to help me and she did, even sooner than she promised.

CHAPTER TWO

ANGELS IN THE OR

"Birth in the physical is death
in the spiritual. Death in the physical
is the birth in the spiritual."
—Edgar Cayce, Reincarnation & Karma

Seventeen hours after my accident, two nurses finally wheeled me in for spinal surgery. A hospital staff member, whose face was only a blur through my tears, asked me to sign a consent form. I've always been a fast reader, but my eyes lingered for a moment on *17 percent chance of death*.

Every surgery has a risk, I thought as I paused. *What choice do I have but to sign it?*

The hallway outside of the operating room was much quieter than the ER, and I considered the times I'd viewed a scene like this on television or in a movie. Being in the scene was surreal, unsettling. The chilly air, greenish gray walls, and florescent lights were exactly what I expected to see, but the tableau made me feel empty and sad. Several people in green gowns passed me and headed into the operating room. Doctor Flawn patted my arm and said, "Let's do this."

I couldn't see the anesthesiologist who placed the mask over my mouth, but I did hear his instructions and counted down from one hundred to ninety-eight while gazing at the ceiling. By ninety-seven, I entered a place where I floated in the blackness of sleep, in the nothingness that I imagined death would be like.

I'm not sure how long the doctors had been at work before my spirit body popped out of my physical form, slightly above and to the right of the operating table. The first moments outside my body felt exciting and electrifying, and my spirit danced a bit of a jig realizing that there is more to existence than the physical. No one, except possibly the most committed atheist, could have been more surprised than me at the onset of my near-death experience. I wanted to pop back into my body, just so that I could tell my agnostic friends that we do go on. I felt certain I could convince them.

Even this first moment of my near-death experience transformed my outlook and understanding. In this environment, I felt like a child again, happy to see what came next and glad that my spirit body retained the essence of who I am. It is difficult to explain what I felt about my physical body on the operating table. I felt some concern for it, but at the same time disconnected from my body. It didn't matter to me if I returned to it or not. My eternal nature made the body somewhat irrelevant and simply a vehicle for the physical experience.

Soft rock music played on the radio, and my back had a long, bloody incision. Surgery appeared more brutal and gory than I had imagined, especially from that vantage point. My vision outside my body was 360 degrees, so I perceived the operating room differently than if I had been physically standing beside myself. I could see above the doctors and the entire operating room all at once without blinking or relying on my eyes.

There, in that space with the doctors, nurses, surgical technicians, and others, I felt incredible joy and awe knowing that an essential part of myself would never die. After joyfully contemplating this first discovery, I noticed two of the most intelligent beings I had ever encountered.

The calm, loving energy they possessed put me immediately at ease. They were very large, approximately eight or nine feet, androgynous with shoulder length hair, and composed more of light than solid form. I refer to them as *angels* only because I have no other terminology that befits what I saw. These angels were part of an enhanced reality and nothing like a dream or a hallucination.

People always want to know more about what the angels looked like. They ask, "Did they have wings?" "Were they clothed?" "How did you know they were angels?"

I don't know if these two beings were angels, in the traditional, biblical sense. I only know that I immediately recognized them as unbelievably intelligent souls whose presence gave me indescribable peace. My own awareness of this new dimension seemed much more limited than their understanding. Most of what I realized outside of my body in the operating room came through immediate impressions, the way a child sizes up whether an adult is trustworthy or not. The angels were trustworthy and there to help and comfort me, so I did not question their authority.

The two angels sent waves of intense light, which transferred many messages to me all at once. The light emitted from the eyes of the angels flowed directly into my spirit body, allowing me to access information faster than the fastest possible broadband speed. Messages were given in the form of completed thoughts and feelings, not individual words. The knowledge they sent into my spirit form not only felt comforting, but it also altered the way I viewed everything about my life.

Though I could not process everything the angels were telling me in that moment, I knew that their communication would be something that helped me throughout my life. These messages would wait inside of me for the right time. The angels wanted to change me so that I would never be as lost as I once was, and they wanted me to help others feel the same peace that they were granting me.

The angels were not only able to interact with my spirit body; they were also able to interact with the doctors, and more importantly, *through* them. The doctors, most likely, did not realize this interaction. I understood that my awareness, my sense of the world, and my ability to experience joy were growing exponentially. Just before the monitor started to beep, signaling that my heart had stopped, the angels slowed down their communication, looked at me intently, and said with force, "*Watch this*!"

They then sent the same light they had beamed into my spirit body through the backs of the doctors, through their hands, and into my physical body. My corporeal form was instantly altered and healed in ways that the doctors might not have been able to accomplish on their own. I knew this to be true because of the information transferred to me from the light of angels. By observing their healing light, I understood that I would regain my ability to walk, that the fragments of bone would be picked out of my spine, that I would feel healthy and alive, and that I would even run again at some point in the future. Light seemed to contain both healing power and knowledge.

As the angels worked on my body, I realized that the surgeons were conduits of their energy and that the angels' energy was an essential part of my healing. Perhaps the surgeons' egos would not be able to hear that or perhaps they would be empowered to recognize that spirit worked through them. I only knew that I needed to remember this moment vividly. The angels wanted me to understand that they could work through *me* in the future. While the angels and surgeons continued their efforts, my physical body shimmered with light and energy.

I have experienced thousands of dreams, but this was more real than any waking moment in my lifetime. In dreams, the dreamer exists in a scenario that feels real, but during the interval that I existed outside of my body I saw a larger, more comprehensive picture, or at least a vast intelligent connection that I had been missing while in physical form. In college, I dropped acid a few times and the hallucinations were minor—more shadowy—nothing like this vivid experience. I had a complete awareness that this vantage point was more real than any reality I had ever experienced in my physical life.

I could never call the angels a dream; rather, their undeniable strength and presence reminded me that I was not alone. The angels saw deeply into me and communicated with me in a more complex way than human beings communicate. Since these two angels had so many messages to relay to me, the term "messengers of God" feels accurate.

From television shows, I had heard what a monitor sounds like when a heart stops beating. I heard that jarring sound, and I briefly saw the surgeons step back while the anesthesiologists and others rushed into action. Through telepathic communication, the angels let me know that it would be okay not to stay in the hospital room.

Now that I had technically died, I didn't want to watch what happened to my body. My spirit form sped through the walls of the hospital, pausing only because I caught sight of my stepdad, Jim. My mom married him while I was in college, and I hadn't really gotten the chance to get to know him. I knew that he made her happy, so I was pleased that she had found him.

I thought he was a health nut like her, so I was surprised when I saw him stopping at the vending machine to buy a candy bar. He pulled out a Snickers bar, always a favorite of mine. In high school, I skipped lunch on occasion just to have a Snickers bar. I thought about how I would probably miss certain foods in this new realm. I didn't know why I spent time watching him, but later I would recognize this would be my verifiable instance outside of my body.

Though I realized I was leaving many family members and friends behind, I felt free, happy, and more peaceful than I had ever felt in my body. Death was not scary, but rather like an exciting trip to a new country—a liberating, fun, new, freedom-filled reality. My spirit body sped quickly through the hospital and out into the night sky above Austin. I thought of the half-hearted prayer I had offered while being transported in the ambulance. I thought about how *I* was free and flying now, much like the bird I had seen before the door to the ambulance shut.

CHAPTER THREE

THE EXPERIENCE OF GOD

"Earth has no sorrow that heaven cannot heal."
—Thomas Moore

In this space of this new freedom, I experienced a connection to God, as if a thread of light ran from my spirit body and connected to wisdom of God. Though far away, I felt that this all-loving, deeply intelligent force was now my guide. The angels had cared for me at first, but now I would be guided by the light of God.

The Austin night sky transitioned into a quick tunnel, and as I journeyed through this tunnel I felt myself being pulled through something that felt comforting and peaceful. Outside of the tunnel, I floated in a warm, safe place filled with stars, and I witnessed a quick life review, which mostly contained the beautiful highlights of my life. Scenes from my life were quickly flashed into parts of a dark sky. The intelligent, loving light didn't want me to relive any pain others had caused me or I had caused myself. Any abuse, neglect, or mistreatment seemed blacked out of existence.

All self-harm, self-loathing, insecurity, and confusion were forgiven by the most loving force I have ever encountered. All the fears and pain of my life seemed to be brushed away, like a cloud that evaporates during the next bright day. These concepts simply did not matter. In fact, I heard the exact words *love is all that matters*, and I saw glimpses of love that I had given to the world. I wished I had given more love. Even smiling at a sad child or talking with a lonely older person in a waiting room held significance, and I saw how much kindness matters.

As the life review continued, I felt a growing understanding and oneness with everyone I had ever known. I had not been a mean person at the age of twenty-two. I was rather shy, insecure, and spent a lot of time reading and lost in my own thoughts and daydreams, opening up and connecting with others only after several drinks. I had disappointed a few people, but I had not hurt anyone deeply.

I saw into the minds of a few of the people that I waited tables with at Tres Amigos earlier that year. They wondered why I did not speak openly with them. I had thought that they were not particularly cool because they were single moms or married and older instead of a university student like me. They did not listen to the same bands or read the same books as me, so I wrote them off. Our only interactions happened around the margarita machine as we filled up sixteen-ounce Styrofoam cups disguised as soda and laughed about how the night became more bearable and the tips flowed more generously the more we and our customers drank.

I realized that I shunned people who were not like me, and that I had failed to notice the compassionate nature of others. Their beautiful hearts were concerned for me, wondering if I might be depressed or sad for reasons they couldn't fully understand. Their kindness was a form of love, and I saw that I had been missing, at the very least, a more pleasant working environment because of my cliquishness and pride. Many times, the loveliest people imaginable might be working or living right beside us and we ignore their struggles, their hopes, and their light because of our own insecurities or arrogance.

After experiencing this connection with a few of my coworkers and others, the light took me back to childhood. I was a sweet child (as most are) and deeply in tune with nature, even able to coax wild rabbits near me as I played in the bushes outside my house. This loving light showed me that everyone needs to spend more time in nature to heal and become whole, more loving and joyful. I saw that most people disconnect from their souls and focus on survival instead of enjoyment and play. Nature can help people to reconnect with their sense of delight and wonder. The light of God seemed to contain limitless love and wisdom.

Just as the angels had slowed down communication to highlight a moment, I heard the words, "Be like a little child. Remind others to love as children love."

I didn't know how I was going to remind others to be like little children, but I acknowledged this wisdom as another lesson I should contemplate on a deep level. If I had to sum up the lessons that were transmitted to me at this part of the near-death experience, I would say that God, or the light, is a loving force that doesn't want people to harm each other and truly desires that we feel joy and happiness in our lives. Love and kindness are the greatest gifts we can give to one another. We are all a part of that light, but we often forget how to love because of fear.

We forget how to walk through this world as the light. We are all closer to God as children because in our innocence love flows more naturally for us. We are gleeful in our interactions with pets, watching a bird in the sky, or gazing into our parents' eyes. We are in love with the world, and the world is in love with us. Most of us breathed easier as children. We lived with a more open and extended awareness, and therefore felt things more intensely.

I had a pure sense of faith as a very young child and connected with God as effortlessly as running through the pine forest down the street from my house or playing with a pet dog. As a child, I had not confused the actions of others with the love of God. God was a loving force connected to my soul. While observing myself a child, I thought about how I had been an extremely loving, forgiving child, and I considered how much better life would be if I still had a heart that pure.

During this life-review, I experienced a much a greater sense of understanding than I had known in my life, and I had a feeling that part of our purpose in physical form is simply to remember our spiritual essence and purpose. While in the afterlife, I wondered how we could ever forget this profound spiritual reality.

As the life-review concluded, my spirit body had taken on the form of a child, perhaps because I was told to be like a little child. I entered a sphere full of wonder and purity, and a blue sky spread high and wide above my view. As a soul, I had an unusual way of experiencing this place. I was not walking or plodding through this environment. Much like the angle in which I viewed my body on the operating table, I took in this heavenly landscape from a 360-degree angle, floating above the scene. The thick grass appeared emerald green and full of vibrant, clear life. I took in the wide, expansive sky, and then focused on the green landscape. Soon, I saw what seemed to a blue pick-up truck that I recognized as my grandfather Clyde's truck.

Clyde was the only person close to me who had died before my near-death experience. A poor country man, he had nevertheless always spoiled me to the best of his ability. I wouldn't have recognized him if not for this truck because he had hair the color of my father's light brown hair. He seemed to be in his thirties, but I had only known him while he was in his seventies with a thick head of gray hair. I had never seen a picture of him at this age, but the angles of his jaw and the look of love in his eyes reminded me of the grandfather whom I had known and loved.

I hopped on the back of his blue Chevy truck, and he drove us slowly closer toward the light of God. My feet dragged the ground through bright clover and grass, light-filled, greener, and more intense than any grass I had ever encountered on earth.

My young-looking Grandpa leaned his head out the window to ask if I wanted to keep going. I nodded yes. Intuitively, I knew where he meant. I have always been an adventurous soul, and I wanted to go deeper into this experience and to merge with the loving light of God. My spirit body headed toward the light by simply thinking that I wanted to go in that direction. At some point, I no longer felt that heavenly landscape, and I journeyed quickly and very close to a love that I cannot describe with words. I have tried to write about this experience so many times, but I break down crying and cannot find the language.

I miss the love. I miss the light. A large part of me never wanted to leave the safety of that place. I felt no stress and more love than I ever imagined possible. I felt more joy and contentment than even the brightest moments this life ever provided, and I did not want to return to my body. No person had ever shown me a love like this love. I had no idea it was possible to feel this good. If a soul could smile, then my soul smiled, and I drowsed comfortably without worry. I felt complete and utter trust in this experience, a full surrender.

As I got deeper into to the light, I actually *felt* the prayers of my mother and father. I thought about how the biological connection is also a spiritual connection. The night before my accident, I had heard my parents alternately crying and screaming in one strange dream after another.

I would fall asleep and suddenly hear Dad's booming voice yell out, "Tricia, watch out!" I would wake up in a cold sweat, wondering why his voice sounded like it was coming to me down a tunnel of time. Then, I would fall back asleep only to hear Mom scream and cry, "No, no, oh God, Tricia, no."

Both of my parents seemed so concerned for my life, and I knew that they were trying to warn me about impending danger, but I could not figure out why. Now, as I heard the reverberation of their terror and fear at the thought of my possible death, I realized that time is relative. On a soul level, both of my parents felt the possibility of my accident the night before, or I had perceived the grief they were feeling now, ahead of time.

I also felt the prayers of my grandmothers, and a couple of my aunts. I especially experienced the prayer of a great-aunt who lost her daughter in a car wreck. I very clearly heard her beg God to spare my mother the pain she suffered when she lost her daughter. This touched me, and I almost wished to return because of her sweet prayer.

I found it amusing that I could not feel any prayers from the most pious and religious of my aunts. I think what I felt more than prayers was their love. I knew who loved me and didn't want me to leave the Earth. I also knew who didn't care if I died, but I didn't judge this information. I understood the wholeness and completeness of experience.

One of the most important lessons transferred to me by the light is that *love is all that matters*. Though this seems like a hippie slogan or a paraphrase from the Beatles, the message felt multifaceted on the other side. Every interaction is meaningless if love is not attached to it in some way. A prayer is meaningless without love. A sermon is meaningless without love. A religion is meaningless without love. Life is meaningless without love.

The prayers of those who loved me felt like a gentle wind, slowing down my progress toward the light. Though the love felt sweet and reminded me of my life on Earth, their entreaties did not suppress my desire to keep going deeper into the light because this was the greatest adventure I'd ever experienced.

As I journeyed more deeply into the expansive presence most profoundly benevolent force imaginable, the light told me to look down and revealed a river. Next to the river were so many other lights that were somehow connected to me. I understood that the lights farther away down the river were farther away in time. I looked down at my own spirit body and saw how large and light-filled it had become. I knew I had become someone different from the fearful, jaded young woman who entered the ER earlier that day, and I saw that God's love is what had changed me.

God suggested that I should return to my body and work as a teacher. The light of God didn't merely suggest that I might become a teacher, rather there were no other options for me. Surely, this intelligent light, a force that loved me this much, had to know how I hated growing up poor and wanted a career more lucrative than the teaching profession. Surely, the divine light knew I was shy and petrified of public speaking. Surely, the light understood I wanted to avoid all traditional careers for women.

After graduation, I pictured myself working as an editor or eventually going into bankruptcy litigation or a type of law that would not require me to speak frequently in court. I had so many questions about the reasons why the light needed me to return to my body and teach, and I protested for a moment.

However, God didn't acknowledge my protest, and the vision of that river would be my very last moment in the presence of God. I wasn't given a second more near a love that is greater than all comprehension. The idea of my life as a teacher seemed etched deeply into my brain, and it was a strangely joyful image, though I didn't understand why at the time.

The truth is, I would've preferred to stay on the other side, but I didn't have a choice. The decision was made for me to return. I felt my soul sucked backward through a dark wind toward my body. Re-entering my physical body felt like being swallowed by a painful, narrowing darkness.

When I awoke, I realized that I had felt more alive while dead. Most of the magic, light, and beauty disappeared, and my body felt heavy, drugged, and painful. I did not want to be stuck in the limited experience of my corporeal form with my history, my stories, my powers of reasoning, my emotional wounds.

Outside my body, I was both myself and greater than myself, connected to a vast flow of information. During that time, I knew much more than I could ever know living in this single, limited perspective. The experience of a more expansive universe made my individual experience seem boring and inadequate. I had witnessed powerful, healing angels. I had glimpsed inside the hearts and minds of family, friends, acquaintances and even strangers in the Austin area. Most of all, I had been connected to the all-loving energy of God. I didn't look forward to only having my limited mind to process life.

CHAPTER FOUR

EARLY RECOVERY

"Death is only an experience
through which you are meant to learn
a great lesson: you cannot die."
—Paramahansa Yogananda

As I recovered in a small white room next to a loud, clanging ice machine, a calm, dark-haired nurse spooned ice chips into my mouth and asked, "What's your name?"

"I remember her name," I replied, still feeling partially connected to the light and greater intelligence I encountered outside of my body. The experience of being only me was disappointing, especially after flying free of physical constraints. In contrast, my body felt dull, hot with pain, and irritatingly constricting. Flight and connecting with angels was much more exciting than being stuck on a hospital bed underneath florescent lighting.

Back in form, I immediately knew that the sensation of being in a body would make it difficult to retain all the amazing connection and freedom I had just experienced. I cried, not because of the physical pain but because I already missed the direct, intense connection to God. Back in my body, it seemed as if all the receptors were muted and dulled. That frequency appealed to me more than this one.

The nurse made me speak my actual name, then I asked when my surgeon would visit me. I couldn't wait to talk to her. When Doctor Flawn finally walked in, I blurted out, "I died, didn't I?"

She looked startled and replied, "We thought we lost you for a couple of minutes, but you're fine now. This is your second blood transfusion, so you'll feel better soon."

Doctor Flawn appeared unnerved by my question, as if I might blame her for my death. As she talked to my nurse, I thought about how traumatic it must be for surgeons to have a patient die on their table because my death was an outcome she wanted to avoid at all costs.

Perhaps she didn't want me to consider her any less of a surgeon. But I didn't. In fact, I felt deep gratitude that she had operated on me and that the angels had worked through her. I only wanted to discuss the moment of my death in greater detail. I hoped that she might be open-minded about near-death experiences and possibly even curious about what I learned on the other side. I wanted to tell her the song I heard playing on the radio and ask if she remembered it. I mainly wanted to tell her about the angels.

I attempted one more question. "So, I was dead about two minutes? How did you revive me?"

Since I didn't see this part of the surgery, I was curious. Doctor Flawn became more guarded and evasive. This was not a conversation she wanted to have with me. She stepped back and said, "You've lost a lot of blood during surgery. You should feel better soon."

Then she walked away quickly, and I was left wondering if my internal injuries caused me to bleed to death. I know my back was open and the incision was a long one. I saw that much from my vantage point above my body.

My spirit form didn't stay in the room long enough to know the answer to these questions, and it didn't look like I would get any answers from Doctor Flawn either.

My grandmother was one of the first people I remember beside me in the recovery room, and Mom was not far behind. I used up my energy desperately trying to connect with Doctor Flawn, so I simply grabbed their hands. Touch felt grounding and brought me back to my painful body.

Later the next day, I let my family do the talking while I rested. When my mom and grandmother talked with Doctor Flawn, she seemed to relax. She was the expert and knew a lot more than they did. Doctor Flawn seemed uncomfortable talking to me now, perhaps because I knew something that she didn't. Mainly, I knew that the angels worked through her to save my life and ensured that I could walk.

Doctor Flawn preferred me as the young woman she met before surgery, someone who was in awe of meeting a female neurosurgeon and openly curious about her education, what part of town she lived in, and what type of car she drove. I went into surgery dreaming of having a BMW like hers someday but came out of surgery wondering how many angels were in the room and if they wanted to work through us.

For the rest of my stay in the hospital, Doctor Flawn appeared busy and rushed, never taking time to engage in extended conversations with me. She stuck to the topic of my physical recovery, emphasizing the success of the surgery; however, I already knew of its success. The success was not completely due to her skills as a neurosurgeon. The angels played a role in my healing.

I stayed in ICU for three days after surgery and often pretended to sleep; however, so many people kept pushing on my stomach, pouring meds into my IV, or switching arms for the IV that sleep was not possible for long. When I closed my eyes, I felt closer to my experience outside of my body. Those first few days, I was afraid I would forget about it, anxious the morphine might wipe away my precious afterlife recollections.

On day four, Doctor Flawn decided I could leave ICU and move to a private room overlooking a small green area of downtown Austin. My extended family of aunts and uncles talked about going to eat at Brick Oven restaurant, and I felt pangs of jealousy because I wanted real food instead of an IV drip.

As a student, I mostly ate Domino's pizza, but I had heard from a few girls that Brick Oven's pizza was amazing. Dad laughed at me when he realized that I was crying about pizza and not my physical condition. He promised that he would buy me a pizza from Brick Oven as soon as I could eat. However, I was crying for more reasons than pizza. I wished my friends were with me, and I didn't understand why only family members were present now that I was out of ICU.

I often cried out of fear, when the nurses lifted and turned me from side to side. I feared losing feeling in my leg again the way I had in the emergency room. I knew the angels assisted during surgery, but I was afraid a human being might mess up my recovery.

On the second day out of ICU, I asked for a pen and paper. My grandmother heard my request and brought me a spiral notebook from the gift store. For a moment, I felt like the young child who adored her, and I remembered her earnest prayers from the other side. I felt deep gratitude and love for her.

The notebook was important to me because I did not want to lose the memory of angels and God's intense love. I felt anxious to put the words down. However, my body was in excruciating, mind-blowing pain, and I could barely keep the pen on the paper. The long black bruises on my arms were fascinating, and I imagined these might have occurred when my arms hit the steering wheel on impact.

My arms were weak, but somehow, I managed to scratch out a few legible lines: "How could I know that the angels I knew only from paintings would become bright, intelligent companions at the end of my bed and that the torrential light from their eyes would answer my questions instantly?"

I wrote the words sideways down the page because I did not have the strength to hold a pen. This sobered me some, as I realized how much pain my body had endured and how much medication must be pumping through my body.

I felt satisfied that I did my best to document my time with angels because I desperately wanted to retain the memory of the other side. My family seemed alien, and I believed that I belonged back in that other realm where communication was much easier and quicker.

I could hear some of the thoughts my family members weren't saying out loud. I had always been a sensitive child and in tune with other's emotions, but this ability seemed much clearer and direct. I wondered if the near-death experience had given me a clairvoyant connection to people. From what I sensed, my mother was mainly concerned about the money; she worried how she and my stepfather would deal with the hospital bills. I told her a few times to stop worrying and that I would have to figure out how to deal with the financials. She looked at me as if I was a child and kept worrying.

Once my dad saw that I could wiggle my toes and realized that I would walk again, the fear and panic surrounding him subsided. He loved me, and we had become much closer once I entered college, often joking boisterously about the latest movies, but I knew he would not be able to take care of me if I became permanently disabled. I saw his relief when he realized that my life would stretch out for a long while ahead of me and that we both would have freedom. Freedom mattered to him more than anything did.

The life of any party and annoyingly optimistic, Dad had a pleasure-seeking skill set that did not include taking care of others. He joked with me, and we continued to talk about all the treats he might bring me as soon as I was cleared to eat solid food. For some reason, I felt like food would make me feel fully human again. I felt part angel, part alien, and part roadkill.

Most of my family members treated me as if I were wreckage, a problem they had to deal with for my mom's sake. They cared for me, but not deeply. Fortunately, I did not perceive my situation like that at all, feeling at times like a sorcerer, able to read thoughts and energy. I knew something powerful had occurred during surgery, and I couldn't wait to read other accounts of near-death experiences which might help me better understand my experience. I had briefly heard about near-death experiences before my surgery, but I had never read an in-depth account of one.

I felt gratitude my family took care of loose ends, like withdrawing me from classes so I didn't fail, but I craved deeper connections with them. They were more concerned with physical details and even took pictures of my totaled car. Obviously, it had crunched up like a light blue soda can, but what intrigued me was how my cocktail tray had wedged into the back of the driver's seat. I wondered if the tray had contributed to my shattered vertebrae.

As a family, they spent a lot of time talking about where everyone was when they got the call about my accident. When I made a final attempt to talk about the afterlife, someone in the room said, "The drugs must really be affecting her brain. I've never heard *her* talk so much about God."

They didn't understand the significance of what had happened to me, or they weren't interested. Whatever the case, I felt marginalized and misunderstood, and my feelings felt raw and childlike. I sunk away from them and concentrated on how the angels promised me that my body would heal. I imagined the healing light they sent into me continuing to work on my broken body. This would become the visualization that would carry me through the many months of healing.

* * *

On the day I was scheduled to get the body cast, a nurse wheeled me into a different area of the hospital. I waited a long while in the cold corridor, certain the morphine had worn off by the time two brash, talkative men wheeled me into the room, stripped off my hospital gown, and clamped me into a metal device that they could rotate while pouring the cast around my body.

One of the two orthopedic technologists brought out something that looked like ordinary pliers and pulled thirty-six staples from my back and hip while I screamed like a person transported to the Middle Ages and stuck in a medieval torture chair.

After that horror ended, the technicians chatted while pouring the plaster on and rolling me in circles like a chicken on a rotisserie.

The mustached, taller of the two technicians said, "The girl we poured a body cast on last week was a stripper and joked that we were covering up her assets and that she wouldn't be able to make a living."

I laughed uncomfortably and asked how she broke her back. The technician told me that she had her accident while bungee jumping off a bridge over Town Lake.

As they continued to pour the plaster around my body, I thought about beautiful Town Lake and how I had jogged those four miles around the lake a week ago. I also thought about how I might've known the stripper. For the previous seven months, I had worked as a cocktail waitress at Expose Men's Club. At least they didn't use the irritating term "gentleman's club."

I didn't come across any gentlemen there, except for a few bouncers who acted like protective brothers. The best of the men at Expose were former professional football players who threw cash at every young woman who walked by, possibly because they knew they were overpaid and the women worked there only to pay bills.

You can learn a lot about your culture by working in a strip club, especially about how some men treat and view women. I started working there because the money Dad promised me vanished in one of his bad gambling bets, and I had to pay rent. After only a few months of working at Expose, I had become rather sardonic and deeply disappointed in human beings.

As the cast grew thicker on my body, I thought about how I wanted to pick better environments to work. I felt sensitive and believed my innocence had returned with the near-death experience. I would have a literal and metaphorical break from my life as I knew it with the chance to relate to others in a more heart-centered, intentional way.

Most of all, I felt more secure and less afraid cocooned in my body cast which fit snugly around me starting at my neck and ending around my hips. When the nurses turned me, I no longer worried. After another day of IVs, I was finally allowed food. Dad brought me a milkshake from Jack in the Box, and the sweet, syrupy milky goodness tasted like manna from the heavens. After over a week with no food, I could not believe how amazing an ordinary milkshake tasted.

Dad and I shared this bonding moment, and then he quickly made an excuse to leave, giving Mom some cash for the Brick Oven pizza as he had promised. Now that I could wiggle my toes and eat, he needed to get back to his own life. I watched him go with some sadness, but I also accepted our interaction as the way things simply were. He would always walk away too soon, leaving me wanting more from him.

CHAPTER FIVE

FRIENDS

"A real friend is one
who walks in when the rest
of the world walks out."
—Walter Winchell

One afternoon, I finally had time alone with my mother, and I wanted very much to describe what I saw on the other side. I hoped that she might be more open to talk about my near-death experience without other family members present. I remember saying, "Mom, I died. I saw the other side, you know?"

She nodded and replied, "Did you see Jesus?"

My heart sank because I knew that she would not understand my experience or be enthusiastic about it if I told her no. I also felt groggy from the medication, tired, and in pain. I wanted to feel someone else's excitement, so I said yes. The Light certainly could have contained the wisdom and beauty of Jesus, even though I did not see a human form depicting him. My yes was a hollow yes. A yes to avoid an argument with her.

The light was lovelier than anything I had ever imagined in Sunday school, and I wanted Mom to understand that we are not judged as her religion claims. After all, I was an insecure, depressed college student; lost, deeply afraid, and experimenting with drugs, but the light had nothing but compassion for me. This amazing divine light gave me deeper, more complete love than I had ever conceived possible.

For so long I had been hungry for complete acceptance, and I found it on the other side. I thought this knowledge might help her too, but she smiled sweetly and patted my hand as if I were only a child, light years behind her in spiritual understanding.

Mom read the Bible to me several times as a child, and I thought about using one of the parables to help her better understand my experience with God. I wanted to explain to her that I was like the loved, prodigal son, and she was somewhat like the dutiful brother, angry that I was welcomed into heaven joyously. I wanted her to rejoice in the amazing reality of that love and feel that forgiveness for both of our experiences. She was wrong, and I was wrong. However, we were equally loved, and I knew this now.

Although I needed to share my experience, I quickly realized that she was not a good audience. After a few moments of talking around the subject of heaven, I asked her, "Can my friends visit now?"

My mother had made the decision—against my wishes—that my friends from the U.T. campus and work would not be allowed to see me until after I got my body cast. I overheard her telling her mother that she wanted to determine whom I could and could not see. It was a typical behavior of hers to take control of my relationships and then get angry that I did not appreciate her interference.

She stiffened and said, "Call them if you want." She walked out and left me alone for the first time. Mom believed I was choosing friends over her. However, I would be staying at her house for months, possibly a year, and this might be my only opportunity to connect with them; so, in a sense, I did choose friends over time with her, and I wished she might have understood or even supported my need for connection with others.

I quickly dialed my roommate, Phil, asking him to remove my bong and take the condoms from my dresser. He said he would take care of those details, and I wondered if my parents had already seen my place. Phil always made me laugh and because he had to find a new residence immediately, I told him it was okay not to visit.

It felt great to hear his voice. Family members asked me several times if Phil was my boyfriend, and I explained each time that he was gay. They could not wrap their heads around that and the confusion, and horror on their faces made me laugh inwardly. Things that seemed normal to me seemed extraordinary to my conservative family members.

The attempted communications with my druggie friends were the most disappointing. One guy called me a downer and couldn't make sense of my accident except for how it affected him. When I explained that I was in a body cast and unable to make it to his boat party, he said, "Well, thanks for being such a bummer. I wanted you to come water skiing and meet some of my friends from out of town."

I laughed, imagining myself in a body cast water skiing across Town Lake. I shook my head at how idiotic he sounded. I honestly couldn't tell if he was joking or if this was how his mind worked. Could he only be concerned with how many girls in bikinis would be hanging out on his fancy boat partying with his friends? Did my suffering mean so little to him? One thing was certain—this guy wouldn't be taking the time to visit me in the hospital. I marked him off my list of friends.

Carey, an occasional lover, promised to come, but he sounded incredibly stoned and out of it. I wondered whether he would be able to get it together in time to visit me. I left a few messages on various people's answering machines and waited.

My neighbor, Nina, showed up first. She walked in quickly, looking back over her shoulder as if she were trying to avoid someone; apparently, my mom told her visitors were not allowed and that she needed to go back home. Fortunately, Nina refused to be told no and asked a nurse for my room number.

Something about Nina's determination to see me let me know that I could confide in her about my near-death experience. Nina seemed open and mature, and though I didn't know her well, I respected her. I whispered, "I saw the other side. I saw angels, and I died."

Nina lit up with interest, and she promised to stay in touch frequently. She held my hand and said with tears in her eyes, "I'm spiritual. I believe in these experiences. I can't wait to hear more about it."

I knew I had a new and important friendship with her, and I felt like my angels had deliberately brought her to me first.

After Nina's visit, many sweet, lively young visitors from U.T., various jobs, and apartment complexes showed up with flowers or movies to keep me entertained. A friend who had been in the hospital herself on several occasions popped in *Saturday Night Fever*, and John Travolta's smooth moves transported me to happier, freer times when large groups of us went to '70s-style parties and dance clubs, not getting home until well after two in the morning.

The upbeat movie playing in the background gave me inspiration to someday saunter onto a dance floor again, celebrating being alive. The conversations were a welcomed break from the largely painful and clinical interactions with nurses, specialists, and the somber mood of family members.

The next few visitors were my friends from Jester dorm—a large, sprawling tower with its own zip-code. I met Cindy and Taylor at one of its infamous tornado parties, a gathering where people circled fast up every floor, stopping for shots on every floor except the so-called "virgin vault," the only floor that wasn't co-ed. Cindy, a petite, extroverted firecracker of a woman known for saying whatever came to her mind, looked at me and blurted, "All week, I've been thinking about how random life is and how something this horrible could have happened to me."

Taylor, a calmer, more grounded girl, looked at Cindy in horror, slapped Cindy's shoulder and said what I was thinking: "Oh my God, this accident actually happened to Tricia, you idiot! We're here to visit her, not to talk about what hypothetically may or may not happen to you."

This lightened the mood as they bickered back and forth, and Cindy rationalized that wasn't exactly what she meant. For some reason, their bantering brought me peace. I smiled at my friends, overjoyed to be reminded of something other than my broken body. It also made me realize how much I had grown up in such a brief time. I knew that the appropriate thing to do would've been to hold my hand and reassure me that I would be okay. Cindy didn't have that maturity yet.

Now, having suffered this trauma, I had that ability. I appreciated the various perspectives of others and simply accepted where they were at a certain moment in time. I understood that Cindy was not able to comprehend another's perspective and existed mainly inside the walls of her ego without seeing the larger connectedness of being human. However, her mind wasn't addled by drugs, and she was grown up enough to be there for me. I recognized that she was more dependable and a better friend than any of my drug buddies. Cindy's presence brought back memories of carefree times—nights of dressing up for Halloween and walking Sixth Street until our thrift-store high heels were ruined.

One night while drinking on Sixth Street, our group lost Cindy, and we ended up finding her because I tripped over her passed-out body on the sidewalk. I sat beside her protectively, laughing and trying to stop my knee from bleeding. I wondered how long she had been sprawled out there and what others were thinking as they stepped over her, not checking to see if she needed help. Our group took plenty of chances with binge drinking, but at the time our behavior seemed normal.

We were living in a bubble of "good times" and cramming for exams, never fully acknowledging how dangerous nights like that could've been. In some small way, maybe my accident was a wake-up call for the people I knew. I hoped they might become more aware of the fragility of life and learn to take better care of themselves.

More people showed up, and the mature, empathetic friends and acquaintances cried for me, held my hands, and showed me the true compassion and love that I needed. They did the best thing anyone could have done: that is to be present, acknowledge my pain and loss, but be strong and open-hearted enough to witness the miracle that I was still alive.

My former coworkers from Tres Amigos also made an appearance, and after connecting with them so deeply on the other side, I made a point to ask them about their lives, their kids, and their work. I felt overwhelming love for them. Their hearts were so lovely, and many of them were Catholics who prayed for me before and after my accident.

They barely knew me, but they cared more for me than some of the fools lost in the drug culture of Austin. When they visited, my mouth felt like cotton and my head was swimming from the morphine. Unfortunately, I couldn't talk with my coworkers as long as I wanted to, but I grabbed each of their hands, feeling incredible gratitude for their presence.

At the end of visiting hours, I begged the nurses to wash my hair before the last group of friends showed up. After a week in the hospital and all the animal panic and fear running through my body before and after surgery, my hair had become matted, sweaty, and greasy. When someone handed me a mirror, I cried out in disgust, hardly recognizing my pink, swollen face.

I looked puffy, bruised, and horrible enough without a filthy head of hair. I'm forever grateful to the nurse who washed the greasy mess. She was off the clock but took the time to help. Often, the small acts of kindness of others moved me to tears. When people do what they don't have to and do so for the sake of kindness, they bless others greatly.

I finally began to sleep better after my visits from friends, and many of my extended family members left and returned to their own families and lives. The last person I still wanted to see was Carey. Since I had stopped using coke the month before my accident, I had seen less of him, but we occasionally hooked up, smoked pot, and listened to music.

At the time, I thought he looked hot in a dark magic, long-haired, tattooed, big-ringed kind of way. I imagined the nurses might be impressed or interested in how I knew him, but I ended up sleeping through his visit. Later, I overheard two nurses whispering about Carey while they thought I continued to sleep.

"I'm glad she was asleep and that her family was out when he showed up."

"He looked scary and freaky. I'm surprised he made it here. He said he could barely figure out the bus system."

"I know. What a druggie."

"Why would a student get involved with a low-life creature like that?"

Suddenly, I felt ashamed and wanted to leave the hospital, hibernate for a while, heal, and think about the light that washed away all the confusion, pain, and darkness of the world. At the same time, even if Carey looked strung out and a little rough, I believed that he deserved compassion, not judgment.

I wanted to see him and tell him about my experience because I believed it might help him. Another part of me thought it was better I had been sleeping. I understood I needed to seek out new friends who didn't do drugs, friends who were aware of spiritual matters. I wanted my life to be different from this point forward, but I also wanted to embrace that part of my past and make peace with it.

I was slated to leave the hospital on the ninth day. Doctor Flawn assured me I was healing on schedule, and I didn't bother attempting to discuss the afterlife with her anymore. Before being released from the hospital, two nurses I hadn't met before informed me that I had to stand up and walk. I begged them to give me more time, but they crossed their arms, and the taller, stronger one insisted, "You're doing this today."

She placed a walker in front of me and pushed me forcibly out of the bed. Since surgery, I had been turned every few hours religiously. They even interrupted my sleep to turn me, but I had not moved myself more than an inch, fearing that I might harm something in my back and be unable to walk. After being in bed for over nine days in addition to the hours spent waiting in the ER, I had no idea what standing would feel like. What I quickly learned is that morphine does not deaden all pain.

Standing felt horrible. My head pounded with universal, expansive pain, pain that seemed to stretch and fill up the entire room. There was no definite place where I began and where the pain ended. It stretched down the hallway that I was forced to slowly navigate with a walker. Older patients, probably in their eighties, passed me as if I were standing still.

When I slowly and shakily made it to the end of the hallway, I saw the U.T. tower and thought about how I might have graduated in a couple of weeks. I held tight to the walker, crying again, unable to deny the wish to go back in time and avoid the accident. Many people yearn to journey back in time after life-altering experiences, and this is one of the few moments I allowed myself to feel a deep grief and self-pity, wondering if I might have chronic pain in my life. I also wished I could've seen the beauty of life and known the existence of a spiritual reality in a less dramatic manner. Since I was stubborn, perhaps this was the only way I would've awakened.

I comforted myself with the knowledge that I did wake up and would no longer relate to people who did drugs or who were completely lost. I knew that my mind was clearer, and my intuition was stronger. I felt altered in a positive way, despite all the physical pain. The day was bright and sunny with a few puffy cumulus clouds, one of my favorite types of days in Austin. If I hadn't been in the hospital, I would have been at Barton Springs, a hidden waterfall, or on a boat on Lake Travis or Town Lake, soaking in the wonders of a Texas spring.

After staring out at the bright day, I considered all the ways I looked at life differently after this week and a half. I thought about the angels, the light from afterlife, and my teaching mission. The mission. I knew I would be returning to campus after physical recovery to get my teaching certification.

I wondered what it would be like to know thousands of students in my lifetime. Teaching was a career choice that I had deemed a back-up plan. I imagined I would teach only if I couldn't find a way to make more money in a different career. Now, teaching was the only plan, thanks to my one-on-one talk with God. With tears still running down my face, I turned my clunky walker around, curious about what my life might become after this experience.

CHAPTER SIX

FAMILY MATTERS

"...Maybe a refusal, any refusal, to be broken lets in enough light and air to keep believing in the world—the dream of escape."
—Jeanette Winterson, Why Be Happy When You Can Be Normal?

A few nurses stopped to say goodbye as I signed the paperwork for my release. I was sorry the nurse who had washed my hair was off that day because I wanted to thank her for her gentleness and compassion. Her kindness was a reminder of the pure love from the other side.

As I looked out my window at a spot of bright green grass, I thought about the heavenly landscape I had seen during my near-death experience. In that moment, knowledge from the other side came flowing back to me. Love was all that mattered and all I had taken with me when I left my body, but I wondered if I could bring any of that clarity into my relationships with my family. Though I was aware of the love God has for all of us, the pain of my body made me all too conscious of being me, and I had emotional wounds as deep as my physical ones.

Knowledge of the expansiveness and unconditional love of the other side that afternoon gave me intellectual peace, but honestly, back in my body I wanted to stay in the hospital. Uncle Darin planned to transport me to my mom and stepdad's house in his station wagon at my parents' behest. Darin and Aunt Jackie, the pious aunt whose prayers were absent on the other side, lived near Mom and Jim. His vehicle would allow me to lie down for the hour and a half it would take to get to San Antonio. Though I appreciated the ride, I wasn't looking forward to it because of my negative history with Uncle Darin.

One of my sweet nurses at Brackenridge Hospital showed up with a bright smile and a wheelchair. She asked if I was ready to go home. I nodded yes, but my heart said no. I wanted to beg her to let me stay.

As she wheeled me toward Darin's station wagon, the sun felt bright and hot on my skin after nine days of being indoors. South Texas can be heaven on Earth or sweltering hot in early May, and that day was a hot one. Two paramedics waiting out front helped the nurses position me on a board in the back of Darin's vehicle. My uncle did not bother talking to me on the drive south on I-35, so I listened to his classic rock music while lost in my own thoughts.

When Darin pulled into my parents' steep driveway, my board slid backwards at an uncomfortable angle. I yelled, "Darin, help me. Please readjust my board. This angle hurts."

Darin scowled at me and left me alone, despite my protests. Hot waves of pain radiated up my spine, and though I screamed for few minutes, no one came to get me. I cried helpless tears, acutely aware of how vulnerable I was and how little control I had over the situation. I felt like a helpless child at the mercy of these same people again.

As I waited in the hot car, the reality of no longer being in college and having to live in my mother's home began to sink in. Though I knew I would be happy never to see Darin again, I longed for a better relationship with my mom. She was many things at one time—self-sacrificing, giddy, easily frustrated, judgmental, disciplined, health-conscious, occasionally cruel, and damaged by her relationship with her own disapproving mother. My grandmother was kind to me, but it was obvious that they had a challenging history together.

Mom tried very hard to make up for her own wounds by loving me in an overzealous way. This worked for a time, especially when I was very young. Mom's sisters thought of her as the long-suffering wife of a very neglectful man and a devoted mom who would do anything for her child.

In some ways, this was accurate, and I did adore my young, funny mother who seemed desperate for my company. She was always with me and sacrificed most of her hard-earned money for my care.

However, no one saw Mom's capricious moods or her indifference to my feelings. Even my dad's parents, who were crazy about their one grandchild, did not see me often because Mom made me get in the closet and hide from their visits.

The isolation of the country felt extreme, as if the wind roaring through the cracks in our eight hundred-square-foot dilapidated shotgun house sometimes roared through my very soul. There were no witnesses to my loneliness. I didn't have siblings or kids in my neighborhood for companionship. I was alone except for the phone and the moon and the stars.

Mom did her best to bring joy and education into my life. She taught me to read before kindergarten and how to love and appreciate nature. We learned a lot of Christian and folk songs and sang these songs in pastures and in pine forests. While spending time in nature, I learned to pray and experienced several moments of great wonder and communion. However, living with my mother was challenging. Mom could switch gears quickly, and I couldn't make connections between my behavior and the punishments she doled out.

Sometimes, when I spilled milk, she simply cleaned it up and looked annoyed, but other times she hit me for my clumsiness. I remember the bruises from one vicious spanking that kept me awake one night in kindergarten. I piled pillows around my body and eventually fell into a fitful sleep filled with dreams of a blind witch who caged me in a small house.

If I tried to fly away, the witch would break my wings with a stick. I could survive and eat because she was blind, but she had power over me. Even at that tender age of five, I woke up and realized the witch in the dream represented my mother, and already I wanted to escape her grasp.

To be fair, I had many wonderful moments in childhood. Mom and I often hiked through state parks and even joined a group of hikers for a weekend trip in Arkansas. We swam in fresh streams and camped in the woods, falling asleep to the sound of crickets, but as the years progressed, she had fewer and fewer friendships which would allow us to get out of the house.

By the time I turned thirteen, I realized Mom was in bad shape psychologically, but I didn't know how to help her. I felt responsible for her anguish, and as our years passed together in that dilapidated home, her depression became increasingly troubling to witness.

When I came home from school one afternoon, Mom let me know that had she read my diary, especially a section where I railed at both of my parents for fighting savagely and never showing each other love or tenderness. Besides laughing at the dog, they didn't have positive moments together.

I wrote down that I wished they would divorce. I wrote that I hated them both and thought they were losers. For pages, I wrote like a chant that might transport me somewhere else, "I hate Mom. I hate Dad." I was tired of stepping around her emotional land mines and watching her yell at Dad until he made his exits, never taking the time to understand what was going on with me. Did she really think that I would write about how much I loved them both?

Mom became even more verbally abusive after reading my journal. She screamed the same hateful words at me that she screamed at Dad, but I did not have a car or an escape route like he did. She yelled my own cruel words back at me, proclaiming her hatred for her only child.

At least once a week, Mom would call me every name in the book and I mean *every name* for doing something as innocuous as turning the channel of the television. She told me that I was lazy and useless just like my dad, despite my straight As and awards at school.

As a young teen, I had no self-esteem and believed I was flawed, mostly because of the way people look at poor families. I grew up poor, ridiculously poor, like Walmart-was-too-good-for-us kind of poor. Poor like I rolled up white bread and ate it slowly when the hunger pangs hit. Poor like I wished my parents weren't proud and would've applied for welfare so that I could eat free school lunches.

Since I wore clothes from tag sales, sometimes kids at school bullied and made fun of me, calling me ugly, disgusting, and worthless. Looking back at the pictures now, I can see I was adorable; a little malnourished and underdeveloped but certainly worthy of love like all children. My innocent soul and compassionate nature allowed me to appreciate all people in an open-hearted way, and I didn't understand why my love wasn't often returned, though I realized that was probably more about them than about me.

One evening, when I was full of despair after a particularly trying day at school, I asked Mom, "Am I pretty at all?" I wanted my mother to tell me that I was beautiful and worthy of the attention and friendship of others. I craved comfort and reassurance, as any young person would.

She admonishingly replied, "You're vain, Tricia. Why do you care about your looks?"

The toll her emotional abuse took on me was immeasurable, costing whatever self-esteem I might have salvaged by the age of thirteen.

Mom mainly blamed her depression on my father's absence. Dad worked in insurance sales and later the sale of retread truck tires. He drove hundreds of miles from Big Springs to Shreveport, sometimes in one day. After work, he spent long hours at the Tackle Shack, a fishing store, hanging out and chatting with the guys about which crankbaits or top water lures worked best for catching the biggest bass.

He must have also spent an inordinate amount of time at restaurants, movies, and bars because he never ate one single meal with us on the home front. Growing up, I couldn't be certain what he did with his time. Most nights he didn't get home until ten or eleven, and Mom and I were asleep by then. Sometimes, I wondered if he had another family.

On weekends, Dad went on fishing trips. The few times we met in passing, usually when he jumped in the shower before heading out again, I'd eagerly show him one of my recent report cards or simply talk about what I had learned in school. He would beam down at me and say, "Keep up the decent work, kiddo. I knew you'd be smart like me."

Sometimes that phrase would be the only kind thing I heard all day, but I longed for something more from him. His overt, upbeat form of narcissism was a welcomed break, but he couldn't be bothered to spend time with me if it interfered with his idea of fun.

Once I entered high school, Mom often threatened suicide with the pistol that she kept in her dresser. At first, I tried to talk her out of these moments, but eventually her suicidal rants terrified me, and I would go for a walk or run, wondering if I would come home to a dead mother, or one capable of killing me.

I understood that her life was difficult. Her soul-destroying jobs at gas stations and fast food joints were demoralizing, and she genuinely wanted me to have better employment and a better marriage than she did. She, like many parents, wanted a better life for me but didn't know how to prepare me for this life because of her own deep well of sadness, pain, and desperation.

For the first two years of high school, I ignored my classmates as much as possible, existing like a timid little specter. I finally acquired a small group of friends during my junior and senior years, and it was a welcomed break to stay out late into the night watching videos at various people's houses. Their lives weren't perfect either, but their houses weren't falling apart around them, and their mothers generally made snacks for us or took us shopping for games and movies.

Since I had a few new relationships, I tried to find help for Mom by asking the parents of various friends about therapists or ministers; however, Mom refused their suggestions, believing she might end up locked in a sanatorium instead of simply talking to a compassionate therapist on a flowered couch. Mom was not always unstable, but I felt unable to comfort her because I needed parenting myself and a peaceful place to live.

Miraculously, my junior and senior English teacher, Missus Platzer, formed a close relationship with me. She encouraged me to write down all my thoughts about my life purpose, the books I read, my parents, my dreams, my wounds, and my wishes for my future. Missus Platzer made me feel safe to share my writing with her, and she pushed me to read challenging works outside of class and complimented my poetry. Instead of fearing my life at home those last two years of high school, I simply put a lawn chair in the backyard most nights and read *Dante's Inferno* until the stars appeared in the sky. I read books by Toni Morrison, Herman Hesse, and even a few spiritually themed books like *The Way of the Peaceful Warrior* and *The Prophet*. Missus Platzer encouraged me to apply for scholarships, something I wouldn't have believed I was worthy of without her encouragement.

Since I had so much pain to escape at home, I had plenty of time to write scholarship essays, and she told me to visualize winning. Though I wasn't at the top of my class, I received a ton of scholarships and the English award from her. Missus Platzer even visited my mother's place of work and asked to her come see me receive these awards, but Mom did not come to the ceremony. Missus Platzer saw me and completely changed my life. Maybe God wanted me to be like her, and I thought if I could reach one young adult the way she reached me, then it was a good thing I came back to my body to become a teacher as God had suggested.

When I left for college, I had endured all I could at home and felt exhausted, as if I had spent my entire childhood swimming upstream. I couldn't wait to make a life far away from Lindale. Before leaving, I took pictures of our ramshackle house. I captured the sinking floors, the sinking roof, the black mildew covering the walls, the religious plaques, the peeling wallpaper, the wood panel, and the mouse droppings. I even took a picture of Mom petting the dog and looking more disheartened than any human being should ever look or feel.

As soon as I settled into my dorm room and attended a few classes, I wrote Mom a letter telling her that she needed to take a chance on herself and leave Dad. I told her that she owed it to herself to try something new. Amazingly, she left Dad and showed up at my dorm on the way to go live at my Aunt Jackie's home.

Mom seemed a little scared, but mostly optimistic and determined. While living in San Antonio, Mom started a new career as a travel agent and met Jim at church. She turned her life around dramatically, but by that time I wasn't interested in knowing her. I was trying to forget the sadness of our life together that was etched into my brain.

I knew that God, at Mom's moment of death, would greet her with as much love as I was greeted with on the other side. I hoped we would have more light-filled moments together and let our past together be released and transformed in love.

* * *

I waited for what felt like twenty minutes in that hot car before Darin, Jim, and Mom came out and carried me into the house. My experience with the prescribed painkillers immediately proved rough, and I vomited every time I took a pill. Quickly, I decided against continuing with them, choosing instead to experience the searing pain, imagining that if I could make it through this pain I could make it through anything else in life.

I took Tylenol and stared at the ceiling, breathing deeply. My stepdad loaned me mellow music and a self-improvement series by Tony Robbins. That afternoon, I chose music because the pain was red-hot and intense. I breathed fire breaths I had learned in a Kundalini yoga class in front of the U.T. tower. To deal with my agony, the breathing seemed the appropriate thing to do.

As I meditated, I imagined a beautiful, crystalline light healing my back. These visualizations seemed real, intricate, and intense. Before the near-death experience, I did not have this kind of connection to a healing force beyond my body.

Still, my body was in a lot of pain, and I waited until the last possible moment to force myself up to use the restroom. I felt like I was walking on swords, like the little mermaid who had been given legs but at an extremely high price. Since I was not steady on my feet, I needed Mom to help me. I called for her late that first night, and she came sleepy and irritated.

My hands were shaking, and I was terrified of injuring my back further with any sudden movements. I freaked out when she tried to position my body over the toilet. I thought I might fall and grabbed on to her to steady myself. Mom got irritated, perhaps fearing I might wake Jim. As I hovered above the toilet, nearly knocking us both over, she hissed, "Shut up, Tricia," and slapped me across the head.

As I hung over the toilet, trying to control my anger, I realized that Mom would have to wipe me. All the many times I felt shock as a frightened, confused, embarrassed child came back to me. I couldn't believe that anyone would be that kind of mother.

After she went back to bed, I cried quietly and begged the angels to help me. Amazingly, I felt some peace as if I was held in a comforting embrace, that all-encompassing love I had never experienced on earth.

Before my near-death experience, I suffered in isolation. Now, my soul seemed to stretch across the night and connect itself to all the kids who had ever suffered at the hands of their parents. I prayed for them and all those in situations far worse than my own. Perhaps being out of body and merging with others reminded me that I was never alone on my journey.

As I prayed, peace from the other side flooded my consciousness, and I knew my focus over the coming months would be to heal quickly and interact with the world in loving, nurturing ways. I grabbed my walker, shuffled as quietly as possible into the kitchen, and found a large plastic cup and napkins. From that point forward, if I needed to pee in the middle of the night, I peed in the cup and then dumped it in the morning.

That solution turned out to be easier than bending to squat on the toilet, and I did not want to risk waking my mother or running into her in the small hallway between the guest room and the bathroom that we all shared.

I put the headphones on and listened to Tony Robbins, writing out his plan for my future success. Robbin's fast pace energized me and kept me focused on positive goals, but I didn't sleep even thirty minutes because of the pain. I wondered whether being a witness to my life, even the horrible moments, might be part of my spiritual journey. I wondered whether these moments would someday help me assist others.

Staying at Mom's house felt like I was reliving my childhood, but in fast-forward with the opportunity to re-parent and heal myself with the help of the angels. I was no longer as emotionally vulnerable, and I could be resourceful in ways I hadn't been as a kid. At least I could see Mom more clearly now with my adult mind and feel compassion for her journey and for mine.

I recognized that Mom was once a sad, confused, lonely little girl herself, desperately longing for her mother's love. Not all parents know how to love, so I chose to love myself more than my mom loved me, and there was some comfort in this. I didn't know how to fully relate to her through my wounds and hers, but I could pray for healing for both of us.

I could also imagine that our souls, released from these bodies, would only remember the love we shared as the only truth. I had felt her prayers on the other side, and I believed that the suffering she brought to my life served a soul purpose. The greatest of stories are those where people rise above tough situations, and Mom gave me plenty of pain to overcome. My soul might have wanted to share a story with others of how to recover from a childhood like mine.

The next morning, I looked in the mirror and said to myself, "You are infinitely loved by God, and you know this now."

I felt connected to a universe of star-laden possibilities. I knew my body would heal, and I knew Mom and I would get along better for the rest of my recovery, mainly because I would not share a single expression of my physical or emotional agony with her. I would keep it all to myself, just as I did when I was a child.

CHAPTER SEVEN

A DIFFERENT KIND OF LIFE REVIEW

"Thank you for the tragedy.
I need it for my art."
—Kurt Cobain

After a couple of weeks, I started to sleep more and most mornings, I woke up amazed at how clearly my mind worked. My creativity and intuition seemed heightened, and I loved being alone with my thoughts. Despite physical pain, I also felt more emotionally balanced than I imagined possible. Being in the presence of God had given me a new kind of peace.

Though my body required a lot of rest, my mind felt hungry for knowledge, and I tore through the books I had always wanted to read, feeling so clear-headed and sharp that it was as if a different soul had returned to take over my body. I wondered whether the new sharpness was because of complete abstinence from alcohol and drugs, a healthy diet, the after-effects of a near-death experience, or a combination of these things. My dreams were often powerful and electric.

Physical pain usually woke me up around three or four in the morning, but I would stay in a meditative state, connecting with the love from the other side and using it to help facilitate my physical healing. I felt the angels continuing to send their healing light into my body, sometimes even seeing molecules of bone growing quickly around the rods in my back.

Mom took a month off from work to take care of me, and each morning she brought me a huge bowl of fresh fruit. She was chipper and full of good cheer most days, and I was grateful for her company. I did my best to engage happily with her, and we never talked about difficult topics. We primarily talked about health and the body's ability to heal.

Mom was eating mostly vegan at the time, and I needed to stay thin since I was constricted to a body cast with only a small hole cut out in the center of my stomach for breathing room. I gladly ate fruit in the morning, lentil or bean soup for lunch, and a big salad with lots of sprouts and nuts for dinner.

Mom praised my strength in giving up the pain meds right away, but the pills made me violently sick so there wasn't much of a choice. In some ways, I felt thankful that my body rejected the pain medicine. I wondered whether the angels wanted me to experience life without substances and learn how to heal myself. The red-hot pain along the incision line and deep in my back often startled me with its intensity, but I felt strong as I used meditation to transcend the discomfort or worked to assist my body's healing abilities.

As I lay in bed reflecting on the last couple of years, the risky choices I had made were hard to recount. I felt acutely aware of how precious and fragile life is. I prayed for my own healing and for all the people I had known. On the other side, prayer felt real, like a wind, and I wondered whether prayer could be sent out to others who suffered as I had suffered. Maybe they might pick up a book or talk with someone who might help them focus on their healing. I hoped that my prayers added to the grace of this world, reaching someone with love.

I thought about a time when I was driving home from waiting tables one evening, wondering what drug I would take that weekend. Marijuana was plentiful in Austin. Mushrooms were fun; ecstasy made me feel loveable, sensual, and ready to dance the night away. Coke pepped me up, making me feel talkative and truly alive; therefore, coke was usually my drug of choice.

Toward the end, however, drugs and alcohol had largely stopped doing their job of cutting my emotional pain. One particular night, my adorable friend, Stephanie, who always wore the best vintage styles, invited me to a party. We drank mushroom tea, but for some reason the tea didn't have much of an effect. Then, we took tabs of ecstasy, but the tabs didn't work either.

We watched a few scenes from *Blue Velvet*, but the movie didn't seem trippy or interesting. Stephanie and I wandered down to Sixth Street, but no bands of interest were playing that night. We checked out Eighth Street, but the club we liked was full, so we sat on the sidewalk and smoked a joint, which also didn't faze us. Sitting there, looking down at our clunky Mary Janes, I felt like I was in a scene of a movie and, over my head, the title read, "The Party is Over."

I didn't know what came next. Law school, graduate school, or taking a random job in a new city were possibilities, but another competing darkness seemed to be at play. I didn't see myself living long if I continued to do drugs, so I quit using them a couple of months before my car crash.

Those long nights in my parents' cramped guest room, I stared up at the water stains in the ceiling and thought about how my life experiences might help me as a teacher. Since God had commanded me to teach, I had plenty of time to think about why this profession might be right for me and what kind of help I could offer to my future students. I imagined that I was not the only child in the world to grow up with a neglectful dad and abusive mom. I imagined I was not the only student who had tried to drown her fear and insecurity in alcohol and drugs as soon as they escaped their homes. I might be able to convince students like me to take better care of themselves.

Some nights, I woke up with a start, envisioning the scene of the accident or some random night full of risky choices. During my life review, the light had viewed me with far more compassion than my judgmental mind did those first few weeks in Mom's house. I had a tough time forgiving myself, but the light flipped through this dark part of my life as if it had very little importance.

Choices made from anxiety and depression were just a shadow. The review slowed down for moments of immense joy and love, especially those times I experienced life in a free and happy way, often in nature or laughing with others. The light focused more on how I interacted, showing me that love for myself and others would make my life better.

In college, the free-spirited part of my life largely felt exciting. I focused on pleasure, attraction, and the creation of funny stories, knowing that we are only young once. However, after a couple of years of intense partying, I found myself longing for a loving, passionate relationship the summer before my senior year. Soon after I noticed this frantic yearning in my soul, I met and briefly dated Jake. I thought all my wishes for deep, intense connection with another person had come true. I don't know if it was him, my fragile psychological state, or the artistic freedom and experiences he represented that awoke such desire in me.

Whatever the case, I was mad about Jake, and obsessed with his dark eyes, his expressive laughter, and the bits of witty conversation we shared. Though the relationship ended badly, I had never let myself feel that deeply for another human being.

During those early weeks of physical recovery, I wanted to look at some of our letters to each other from my new perspective. I had carefully saved a letter and short story from Jake in a shoebox in the apartment complex my parents cleaned out. Jake was a common breed of slacker from the mid-nineties who graduated from USC with a philosophy degree and ended up in Austin via picking grapes in Australia, making furniture in Barcelona, and drinking a lot of cheap beer in Prague. Our talks about art, opera, and great authors were a form of heaven to me. The afternoons we spent making out in the grass were the happiest moments of my young life. Once, six hours flew by and it seemed like we had been in each other's arms only a few minutes.

I wanted to see his writing again, mainly because I was curious whether I would still think he was a great talent in my clearer, less drug-altered state of mind. When Mom returned to work, I asked her to bring me all the papers from my apartment, especially the papers in the box in my closet. I feared she would look at a love letter and passionate short story written for me and throw it out.

My fears were correct. Jake's letter and short story were trashed. I would never get to see whether I imagined his genius or if he truly had talent. I remembered telling him that I thought his work was as good as any Hemingway, Carver, or Bukowski story.

Jake and I met in August and he broke up with me in early November of my senior year. We continued to have sex when I knocked on his door heartbroken and often drunk. I hoped he would change his mind about the breakup, but he continued to pull away from me emotionally. After I returned from a disastrous trip to L.A. that I took in the hope of getting over him, I called him immediately.

I had left my car with Jake since he didn't have one, and when I returned I called him. Jake told me he had left it at a friend's house which was walking distance from my apartment. He talked to me as if he had rehearsed this particular speech and said, "I don't ever want to talk to you again. I had a dream the other night, and in this dream, I told you to fuck off. In the morning, I woke up and felt great."

I slumped to the floor and listened a while longer as tears streamed down my face. Jake continued with his rant and said, "Your life is dark, and I don't want to be around to see all the bad things that will happen in your life. I hate you, especially the drug use. I hate being around you. The way you live disgusts me."

He might have continued railing at me, but I hung up the phone to howl in pain. I felt convinced that I had only been experimenting. I consumed exactly one wine cooler and had an amazing grade point average my freshman year. I knew I had gotten off track in college, but I didn't want to believe that I was a lost cause. I wished that Jake had insisted on counseling or a recovery program. I would've done anything to hang on to his love, but he left me stranded in a well of loss, self-hatred, and horrifying confusion.

The next day was Christmas Eve, and I couldn't bear to see my family. I wanted to create a life and love better than my parents had experienced, but I had failed at making a deep and meaningful connection with someone who I wanted. I called Mom to say I was staying in Austin. In my darkest moment, I knew I would have only received judgment from her.

My roommate, Phil, had left earlier to visit his parents. With the place to myself, I decided there was no reason to live. I felt like no one in the world could help me, and I was certain that I had experienced the deepest love I would ever feel for another human being. In that moment, I believed that everything moving forward would only be a form of pretending.

Phil had a half-bottle of Vicodin from a trip to Mexico, and I had a nearly full bottle of painkillers from my wisdom-teeth extraction. I gathered every pill in the house; for courage, I drank the one bottle of wine we had in the apartment. I thought about all the silly times Phil and I had cooked together, often making spaghetti or pizza.

I would miss Phil and a few others, but I didn't know how to move through the pain of losing Jake. I didn't imagine he would even know that I had died. I assumed Jake would continue with his life, never bothering to wonder about me. I felt braver than my mom who had only threatened suicide; I felt like the real deal. In these swirling, painful thoughts, I swallowed handfuls of white pills, chasing them with the half-bottle of whisky Phil had carefully poured into a glass decanter and placed on the dry bar.

I felt certain these would be my last moments on Earth. The apartment quickly closed in on me, becoming soft and hazy. I vaguely remember making it to my bed, despite how slowly and heavily my heart was beating. I fell across the bed face down.

Thirty-six hours later, Phil came back from his parents' house, and I woke up to bright sunlight on one of those winter days in Texas that feels like early summer.

I had intended to die, and it seemed anticlimactic to wake up in my own dried vomit, wondering if the balcony door had been opened the entire time or if it blew open at some point. I crumpled up the suicide note and quickly washed my face, not bothering to explain what I had done. There was no near-death experience, no angels, and no insight. That day, I woke up lost as I had always been.

As I reflected on this after my near-death experience, I wondered what purpose that experience had for me. I imagined it might make me more empathetic to my students who were hurting after breakups or suffering from depression. Maybe I could become for them what my mother could not be for me. I would suggest rehab, counseling, and other services to people who were hurting. I would not scoff at church, either—any avenue could lead to their healing, as long as it was right for that person.

After a lot of time alone with my thoughts, I longed for a different person's perspective. Whenever Mom left the house to grocery shop and run other errands, I immediately picked up the phone and called Nina, my first visitor from the hospital. We spent hours talking about her heartbreak over her long-time girlfriend, Teresa, and mine with Jake. We talked about our exes so frequently that our discussions bordered on a part-time job.

Eventually, Nina and I reached the end of our purging and poked fun at ourselves. I hadn't had a best friend like her in years, and I credited the near-death for giving me a greater potential for intimacy. I felt proud of my new capacity for deeper friendships. Nina listened to the story of my suicide attempt with empathy and even made me laugh about her own botched attempt in high school.

She jumped off a bridge but landed on the asphalt on the side of the bridge and slid on her stomach all the way down to the freeway. A random car stopped to help her, and that stranger drove her home. Her face was badly scraped on one side, and the driver kept asking her whether she needed to go to the hospital. She shook her head and thanked him, pretending the fall was clumsiness on her part. Though our attempts at self-harm were serious and could have ended tragically, Nina and I were still able to laugh at ourselves, and this let us feel that we would continue to survive.

When I thought about returning to Austin and finishing the classes I needed to graduate, I wanted to go back and do everything differently. I saw how lucky I was to have survived my suicide attempt and hoped that I would be the type of person to be there for many others in their times of need or desperation.

If I had reached out to a friend or acquaintance, I probably wouldn't have made the choice to take all those pills. I didn't need to feel like Jake or anyone had enough power to make me feel worthless. His opinion of me was only his opinion; and besides he only saw one snippet of my life, not the extended cut.

I wanted other people to know their intrinsic value. God saw tremendous value in me and loved me with a fervor that made me feel newly born. Everyone on Earth needs access to this love and acceptance. Heaven isn't a college that requires a high grade-point average; rather, it is a place of deep healing and a place to remember all that is divine and holy about being alive.

I imagined returning to Austin while focusing on how to love myself better and treat myself with respect. I wanted to work out more, do yoga more often, and enjoy the outdoors. If I met Jake or anyone knowing what I knew after my moment with an all-loving God, they would see a much more light-filled person. I might not even choose to know someone like him, much less fall in love with him.

I couldn't help feeling more hopeful about my life. I looked forward to getting my teaching certification as the light had commanded. Not everyone can say they had God as a career guidance counselor, but I had a specific mission, and my life had a far greater purpose than falling in love, feeling passion, and getting my heart broken. I was created to help as many students as possible realize their worth, their light, and their goodness.

Possibly, I could also help a few students traverse difficult passages in their lives with fewer scars than me.

CHAPTER EIGHT

LONG, HOT TEXAS SUMMER

"If you have the ability to love,
love yourself first."
—Charles Bukowski

Spending that summer in South Texas while encased in a body cast had challenges. In late June I started walking for physical rehabilitation, but I wanted to avoid sweating inside the cast. I forced myself to get up at dawn, the only cool part of the day. At first, I could only shuffle a few feet past the mailbox, but after a few weeks I made it halfway down the street. A few retired couples who drank their coffee on their porches watched my progress, and I chatted with them about their lives, their children, and grandchildren. They were all curious about my accident.

Sandra, who lived opposite my parents, told me how she was diagnosed with breast cancer a few years prior. When I told her about my near-death experience, and the angels I met on the other side, she grabbed my hands with tears in her eyes.

Before my near-death experience, I barely knew any of my neighbors except for Nina, but now I knew a half a block of people. As I made my slow journey each morning, casting a strange shadow in my bulky body cast, huge T-shirt, and large, wooden walking stick, I felt the neighbors' prayers and well wishes. Many times, I had to stop and catch my breath from a sharp moment of pain and gear myself up for a few more steps.

After my morning walk, I waited impatiently for Mom and Jim to leave for work. Once they both left, I turned the air conditioner up to avoid sweating and exercised, or at least paced through the house, listening to the radio or to some of my stepdad's classic rock records loudly. The muscular calves I had from training for the 10K atrophied during the days I spent in the hospital, and I could barely stand on my toes. I had a long way to go before I fully regained my strength.

Week by week, I checked off titles of books that I had always wanted to read but had never before had the time. I tore through *The Brothers Karamazov*, *The Kreutzer Sonata*, and *The Metamorphosis*. Then, I moved on to the Americans and read *Gravity's Rainbow*, *White Noise*, *An American Tragedy*, and *The Ugly American*. I wasn't sure where to begin with spiritual teachers, but I started with *Saved by the Light* by Dannion Brinkley. His book lit me up, as did books by Raymond Moody. I wanted to call both men because no one I knew could understand my experience like these two, but I wasn't sure that either would take my call.

By happenstance, I came across an article about Carlos Castaneda and asked Mom to pick up every book the local library had including *The Teaching of Don Juan*, *A Separate Reality*, *Tales of Power*, *and The Art of Dreaming*. Brinkley and Moody gave me the confirmation I needed about my experiences of the other side, and Castaneda introduced me to the idea of dream control.

For an entire month, I stared at my hand, willing myself to see my hand in a dream as my cue to begin lucid dreaming. After weeks of practicing, I had a dream where I was on a date with a guy who drove a red Ferrari. I have never cared much for flashy, red cars, so I got out of the car and slammed the door. When I did, I slammed my hand in the car door. My hand hurt, and I looked down and stared at my damaged hand. This moment became my anchor in the dream so that I could begin lucid dreaming.

I waved happily to the guy and shot up into the sky like a superhero with a mission to eradicate all suffering. Flying felt amazing, just like it had when my spirit left my body and flew through the walls of the hospital and out over the night sky in Austin. I flew in large, relaxed circles above the ground, looking down at our beautiful world and feeling wide expansive freedom of an eagle. From this vantage point, I thought about how most people on Earth desire love and money, so my mission started by giving everyone gold as a symbol of abundance.

As I flew around the world, I made sure that no one felt hungry or lacked shelter. I spread joy and light into everyone's heart. Those who desired a companion, a community, a great love found these connections, but they loved themselves deeply as well, knowing that to commit to another takes strength. Most things and people leave us in one form or another, so I gave everyone love and strength to be their own spirit guide, to love themselves deeply and to guide themselves home.

Since I still had time in the dream, I wondered what I wanted on a hedonistic, pleasure-seeking level. I decided to make love to four different men that night—Johnny Depp, Antonio Banderas, Andy Garcia, and Matthew McConoughey. The making love part was not played out in detail and was more of a soul merging of sorts. It left me feeling satisfied nonetheless, and in the mood for a celebration. I wanted the lucid dream to continue, so I crashed a wedding in a castle and watched the young, happy couple exchange happy vows in this fancy, festive setting. Afterwards, I ate a huge piece of a thickly frosted wedding cake.

I thought about what would make for a perfect ending to a wildly fantastic dream and decided that I wanted to feel the creative power of being a great composer. As I flew through the pink clouds of sunrise, I imagined that I wrote every note of Mozart's Magic Flute, deeply pleased with what it must have felt like to be a musical genius with the ability to create such happy, joyful sounds.

When I woke up, I felt incredibly happy. This lucid dream proved one of the most exhilarating moments since my near-death experience. Though I didn't fully understand manifestation, I gathered from reading Castaneda's books that a lucid dream meant I was on the right track to controlling my reality, so I began working on manifesting something small, as a test. In the same way that I had studied my hand to work on dream control, I picked a random image and pictured a guy with dark curly hair wearing a hat like the one Walt Whitman wore in his jaunty frontispiece to *Leaves of Grass.* I pictured him walking up to me in a crowd and asking, "Are you from Austin?"

I would reply only, "Yes."

If I could manifest the random guy in my reality, this would be an indicator that my mind and imagination had some control over reality. I imagined that it might take a while to manifest a moment because it had taken me a month to experience one single moment of dream control. I was curious about how much effort it would take to manifest a small moment in time.

On nights when I tired of reading and couldn't sleep, I decided to work on blessing everyone I had met or briefly known starting with those in Austin and meditated in a way that might send out loving energy and blessings. I was also simply happy to be alive and wanted my good energy to be experienced on some level by everyone I had known, however briefly. I started with my mom and Jim since they were kind enough to open their house to me.

Then, I thought about a particularly memorable class at U.T.—Contemporary Moral Problems. The two professors who taught this philosophy class drew a crowd with fascinating lectures. One suit and tie-wearing professor took the conservative approach to moral problems and the other flip-flop wearing, longhaired professor took the liberal approach. They were close friends and hung out together on campus. During lectures, they discussed problems in society that affected our student population and seemed genuinely worried about their students' welfare.

I also sent love and blessings to the instructors I didn't care for like the sexist instructor of The Major Writers of the Eighteenth Century. My friend, Raj, and I studied together and often wrote our papers side by side in the Perry Como Library, running ideas by each other and checking each other's work. One afternoon Raj read my paper and said, "Honestly, I don't understand why I keep getting an A and you get a B on every paper. I think you did a better job on the last paper."

After a bit of convincing, Raj agreed to put his name on my paper, and I put my name on his paper. I felt certain that the instructor would give me a B when he saw my name at the top of the paper because of the way he treated me. I sat in the front row with Raj, and we both raised our hands to answer all the questions about Swift, Defoe, Voltaire, and our favorite writer, Goethe. The instructor let Raj finish his points, but cut me off mid-sentence, condescendingly continuing my thought as if I were incapable of making a point.

I decided I would not come into the classroom with stereotypes and judgments. I would give each of my students a chance to prove themselves no matter what style of clothing they wore, no matter their gender, their race, their nationality, their age, or their sexual orientation. Raj received an A on my paper with his name on it, and I received a B for his paper with my name on it. Raj looked visibly relieved that his grade was not compromised, though we later talked about how it was sad that we couldn't call the guy out for his bias.

I thought fondly about a girl in my linguistics class who wore cool hats. We planned to meet and study for the final exam the day of my accident. I didn't have her phone number, but I felt certain we would become close friends after studying and chatting about our plans after graduation. She had a certain light about her that made me want to know her.

As I thought about students and professors I'd known at U.T., I envisioned the kind of instructor I wanted to be and the kind I didn't want to be. I remember asking a Psychology professor at the end of the semester if she might bump my grade of a 78 percent up to an 80 percent. I told her that I had a rough semester with several personal issues. She seemed jolly and upbeat, ready to hit the ski slopes in Utah over the holidays. Without a second thought, she gave me the two points, and I bounced out of her office, a little more excited about the holidays myself.

I promised myself that I would make students happy whenever possible, doing my best to love them the way the light loved me, even if this love was given only in a brief smile or a word of encouragement. I would not judge students who were in pain, and I would try to give them helpful suggestions.

I sent love to all the people who kept me up in the dorm rooms, playing their music too loudly, partying, even on a Monday night. I sent love to the homeless people who hung out on The Drag, and the kids who pretended to be homeless. I sent love to the people who sold bagels and the baristas who made my cappuccinos at Quackenbush's coffee house, a shop on The Drag near the famous frog "Hi, How Are You?" mural, created by Daniel Johnston. Kurt Cobain made that image famous, and when I heard of his death a couple of weeks before my accident I rested on the ground in bright, sunlight area of campus, looking at the clouds as a way of paying tribute to him.

* * *

That summer, I received several letters and phone calls from friends and acquaintances. Anyone kind enough to write or call received my full attention. Besides light exercise, meditation, and reading, I had few other distractions. In college, I had participated in a couple of writing groups. Though I was not attracted to the men in those groups, I felt grateful for the books they sent, the cards, and the phone calls.

According to the International Association for Near-Death Studies (IANDS), one of the aftereffects of near-death experiences is an ability to be fully loving to many different people, openly generous and "excited about the potential and wonder of each person they see. Their desire is to be a conduit of universal love." Although this ability later worked great in the classroom, I opened myself up to unwanted attention those first few years after my experience.

I spent hours listening to various people's tales of loneliness or romantic troubles. Nathan, a well-known poet in Austin, and twenty-five years older than me, had recently been given a year to live due to lung cancer complications. I hoped that my knowledge of the other side gave him peace about dying.

One night I picked up the phone and Nathan sounded quiet. The woman's voice on another line said, "Is the little bitch on the line?"

Nathan whispered, "Yes."

Shelly picked up another line and said, "Nathan, tell her that you love me."

Nathan sounded like a robot when he said, "I love you, Shelly."

"Tell her that you don't love her," Shelly snapped.

"I don't love you, Tricia," Nathan said quietly, and I realized that he probably had fantasized about me. This situation felt ridiculous to me because I wasn't interested in him, and I thought that my body cast should protect me from all romantic drama.

Nathan called me again the next day, telling me how Shelly had looked at the phone bill. I reminded him that he needed her help and should be kind to her, and he reminded me that he was leaving her his house.

That evening, a still angry Shelly called but Mom picked up the phone and talked with her. Shelly asked Mom what she would do if her husband spent hours talking on the phone to a twenty-two-year-old girl.

Mom can be silly at times, and in a high-pitched, girlish voice she giggled and said, "Well, I'd invite her over to dinner to see what was so interesting about her. I trust *my* husband."

Apparently, Shelly didn't like Mom's response, but Jim and I couldn't help laughing. During dinner, they teased me for bringing drama into the household, and we laughed and joked about all the ways we could torment the couple. Jim is good at impersonating different people's voices, so he came up with a fake female's voice and said he would pretend to be Nathan's telephone girlfriend if Nathan would leave him the house. Mom and I laughed at his silly impersonations.

I felt some healing watching Mom and Jim have fun together. I had never observed her in a happy relationship, and I felt grateful to be a part of their dinners. Though I thought about being more careful about who I befriended, I couldn't help seeing the possibility and light in everyone, and I felt sad that Nathan and I couldn't be friends who chatted about poetry and death.

Another guy, Blake, from the same writer's group called frequently, and I could tell he had a crush on me. Tall, blonde, and broad-shouldered, Blake looked like he could play a doctor on television. Sadly, I didn't feel the same attraction for him, and the bitterness he felt about his ex-wife repulsed me. I wanted him to heal though, so I talked about my near-death experience with him. He enjoyed these types of discussions, and he told me about how he had tried to induce an out of body experience in his lonely teenage years. When he sent me a couple of CDs, and a drawing of our naked bodies meeting in a lucid dream, I knew I had to be honest with him about my lack of attraction for him.

Initially, he was upset and said I should look for more of a soul connection than a physical one, but I countered that I didn't feel my soul's destiny would be with him either. He called and apologized the next week and let me know he would be moving to Iowa City. Inwardly, I felt a surge of anger that he picked Iowa City because I knew that city housed one the best graduate writing programs in the country. I figured if I had to teach, I could eventually teach at the college level. Something told me that I wouldn't be applying to that graduate program if Blake lived there, but I wanted to believe otherwise.

Blake seemed to want something more from me that I didn't want to give him, and I wanted something from Jake that he didn't want to give me. We were all looking for our souls in another person and not realizing that our connection to the divine offered a true source of pure happiness. I knew this on the other side. No one accompanied me there, but I was whole and part of the loving, forgiving divine. I didn't need anyone there and I didn't feel alone. When we forget about our connection to source, we are sometimes reminded of this spark of the divine in another.

When I first met Jake, I noticed that he lived closer to his essence than I did. Now, I had what I saw in him in spades. In fact, I was little more than pure, vibrating consciousness. Most nights at my parents' house, I felt disconnected from the material world and lived fully on the light from within. Though I knew Jake did not want to hear from me, I wrote him a letter anyway, briefly describing my accident and near-death experience. I remembered images of Jake walking around his apartment and cracking me up with his wild sense of humor. I hoped my letter might give Jake a glimpse of my transformation and allow for a different closure for us.

When Lane, a friend of mine from philosophy class said he felt like taking a long drive and promised to swing by my parents' house in San Antonio, I persuaded him to give the letter to Jake. I didn't know Jake's new address, but I knew the restaurant where he worked as a cook.

Lane hung out with me for a few hours, and we drove to a nearby grocery store so that he could pick up snacks. Though only a few afternoon shoppers were around, I didn't feel prepared for their stares at my large body cast and walking stick decorated with feathers. Children pointed at my body cast, and even an elderly woman in a wheelchair squinted at me quizzically.

Lane picked out a few different candy bars for his trip back home, and as I pushed the shopping cart back into its place, the glare from the florescent lights on the metal reminded me of the stretcher in the ER. For a split second, my spirit popped out of my body, floating somewhere near the ceiling for a few seconds. These moments of popping out my body were disconcerting.

Lane finished paying for his candy and offered me his arm for support. He stayed for a while at Mom and Jim's house and we talked about Austin and all the good times we had shared there. That afternoon he told me about his plans to move to New York.

A few weeks later, Lane called me to tell me he was packed up and ready for the long, cross-country drive. I asked if he gave the letter to Jake, and he sighed. I knew the news wouldn't be good.

"Listen, Tricia, Jake's a real asshole. I never got what you saw in him. I'm not going to sugarcoat what happened. I found him outside the restaurant where he works, and I told him you were in a very bad car wreck. He glanced at your note and said, 'She never was a very good driver.' That's all he said."

I laughed it off, agreeing that Jake was indeed an asshole, but when I hung up with my friend I grieved in a way I never allowed myself to grieve. My rational mind knew Jake was not worthy of my infatuation, but I couldn't help wanting connection. Jake would never know me as my purer, more childlike, blissful self.

Many mornings, I woke up and looked with joy at a robin in the tree beside my window or spent an hour staring into the baby blue eyes of a kitten one of Jim's workers scooped up out of the middle of a traffic jam. Though more of a dog person, a shy, scared kitten suited me better at this stage of my recovery. I named the tiny kitten Crystal, and she perched and purred on top of my body cast, seeming to send me white threads of divine love and healing. We were one, and the love I had for life, even the smallest moments, carried me through most of my days.

I sent all the overflowing love I had in my heart into my own heart. The love I had been sending to Jake and the people I had briefly interacted with in Austin, I focused on myself for a while, observing the waves of emotional pain until they subsided. I gave myself the respect and attention I wanted from him, from my mother, from everyone who had hurt me. Eventually, I cried a whole lot less and laughed a whole lot more. I focused on my future, especially the idea of teaching, imagining how I might try to be as good as some of the best instructors I experienced and much better than some of the worst.

Every day, I tried to improve my physical strength and healing in some small way and by late June, I finally made it to the end of the street. This felt like a huge accomplishment, like I was less of a large, wobbly toddler. Some of the neighbors were out on their porches, so I lifted my walking stick like I had just hiked to the summit of a tall peak. Two sets of couples stood up cheering and clapping for my progress. They yelled, "You did it! You did it, girl!"

Their standing ovation energized me. I smiled and waved at them, feeling like I was a medalist in the Summer Olympics instead of a young woman in a body cast, lucky to be walking and above ground. Something I had taken for granted—walking to the end of a street—now seemed cause for great celebration. I had an extra serving of fruit salad that morning and turned up a classic rock station loud enough to hear from the patio. My life felt peaceful and good.

CHAPTER NINE

VENTURING OUT

"The trick is in what one emphasizes.
We either make ourselves miserable,
or we make ourselves happy.
The amount of work is the same."
—Carlos Castaneda

That September, I watched the school buses drive through the neighborhood and I felt a deep longing for the classroom. That was the first September I had not been in school since kindergarten, and I felt acutely aware of how much I always enjoyed school. All the school supply ads in the newspaper and the back to school commercials on television caught my attention. After a while, I found comfort realizing that I would probably spend most my life on a teacher's schedule and this might be my only break during this time of year until retirement.

I savored the time off by taking plenty of naps and cut down on my obsessive reading schedule, choosing to watch a few episodes of *Oprah*, *Frasier*, and *Seinfeld*. I preferred comedy and couldn't handle more than one episode of *ER* because of the sound of the sirens and the visuals of the stretchers. The first time I heard a siren and saw a stretcher, my spirit popped out of my body and hovered somewhere near the ceiling. This was not a pleasant out-of-body experience because there seemed to be no reason for it other than my spirit was loosened from my form and reacting to the memory of physical trauma. I wasn't sure how to soothe myself through such reactions and assumed that time might heal my response, so I stuck to comedy, relishing the silliness of Frasier's proclivities.

When Mom and Jim left for work, I claimed more of the house, lying on the carpet and practicing stretching my hamstrings like I'd learned in physical therapy. I'd put on some of Jim's vinyl records. Mom didn't care for rock and told me that she walked out of a Jimi Hendrix concert in high school because she thought the people at the concert were weird. When I heard that, I wished I could go back in time and take her place at the concert. I never tired of "All Along the Watchtower," no matter how many times I heard it.

For most of my childhood and early adolescence, the only music allowed in the house was classical or Christian music. Once I arrived in Austin, I had a lot of catching up to do from the music of '60s and '70s like Pink Floyd, Led Zeppelin, The Doors, Ray Charles, Creedence Clearwater Revival, Bob Dylan, Miles Davis, Cream, and Leonard Cohen. At my parents' house, I enjoyed some music I hadn't heard before, like Phoebe Snow, Kraftwerk's *Autobahn*, and Jean Michel Jarre's *Oxygène*. These peaceful songs allowed me to continue visualizing physical and emotional healing occurring inside of me.

One afternoon, while listening to Emerson Lake and Palmer's "From the Beginning," I looked up at the ceiling fan spinning above me. Though it looked the same as always, I saw a flash of it falling from the ceiling and landing on me. I thought I might be developing needless paranoia, but I got up anyway and walked to the kitchen for a glass of water. As soon as I walked a few feet away, the ceiling fan fell and landed exactly where I'd just been.

I appreciated the warning, but I was also disturbed by this newfound power, fearing that psychic flashes take over my reality. How could I function in the present moment if I received too many flashes about the future? I imagined that an ability like this would mark me as strange among my peers.

At the time, my only concept of a psychic came from the signs I saw on small houses filled with crystals on the side of a busy freeway. Out of curiosity, I had visited one of these types of psychics in high school with a group of friends, and her predictions for us all were eerily correct. Still, I assumed that most psychics didn't know lottery numbers, so I wondered about the relevance of my new gifts. Why know a few random things and not others? I assumed that these psychic flashes would diminish as I got farther away from the near-death experience.

Part of me longed to return to the normalcy of being a college student, and another part of me wanted to fully embrace my spiritual experience and move somewhere like Sedona or Peru, wondering what it would be like to meet a shaman who might teach me to be more in touch with the earth and work with guides. The light left me with the impression that I needed to be a teacher though, and I interpreted that message in the traditional sense of the word.

Most days after Mom got home from work, she spent time chatting with me, and early on in our discussions, Mom confirmed that Jim had returned to the waiting room with a

Snickers candy bar. Jim left the waiting area because my dad showed up. The meeting was awkward, so Jim let Mom have a few moments alone with Dad. When Jim left, Mom said she was struck with a feeling that I might die, so she got on her knees and said a prayer for me. When Jim walked in with the candy bar, he interrupted her prayer by saying something silly and they all laughed. Outside of my body, I stared at Jim for a while, wondering about the significance of the moment. Later, this moment proved my verifiable detail, a detail that caught the attention of researchers who study veridical perception in near-death experiences.

When Mom confirmed the moment, she seemed genuinely excited about my experience. However, she quickly began to vacillate between excitement and disbelief after she talked with her minister. Eventually, she sided with him, a man who had not had a near-death experience himself. Mom brought home a homemade pamphlet from her church that claimed near-death experiences were from the devil. As evidence, it cited a minster's wife divorcing her husband shortly after her experience. I couldn't understand why my mother couldn't recognize that something special had occurred in my life because I knew that I would forever resonate with the love I experienced in the afterlife.

The angry font and images of that pamphlet screamed fear. Clearly, that minister's wife was simply filled with love, empathy, and connection to others. She became too open-minded for her fear-addled husband and could no longer resonate with judgment; probably she imagined that if a religion different from his Baptist religion preached a message of love, then it might be closer to the truth.

Love is all that matters is what I clearly heard on the other side, and I imagined that this love could be found in a

Catholic church, a Methodist church, a Buddhist temple, a Hindu temple, a mosque, synagogue, or in a group of people meditating together. I'm sure this minister's wife knew that love is the most important message of a spiritual teaching, but my mother's minister thought the divorced woman was going to hell, and he convinced my mom that my experience was of the devil because I didn't see a physical representation of Jesus. I did hear the words "be like a little child" and this had to come from the wisdom of Jesus, and I also felt a great innocence enter my being at that point in the near-death experience.

However, to some Christians, if a near-death experience doesn't exactly mirror the Bible, then the experience is immediately branded a lie. I wanted to argue with Mom now that I was getting my strength back, telling her that the love I felt on the other side could not be wrong. If God chose to communicate with me through a light instead of the physical form of Jesus, then that was simply my experience of God.

Maybe *she* would've been more comforted by the image of Jesus and would've felt God through that form, had she gone through what I experienced; perhaps a loving God comes to us in a unique way that brings us each peace.

* * *

Earlier that summer, I entered a writing contest I saw advertised in the *San Antonio Express News* for the First International Poetry Festival, and in September, I received notification that I had won second place. I was invited to read my poem at this event which promised to include special appearances from the well-known poets San Antonio poets Naomi Shihab Nye and Sandra Cisneros. I felt overjoyed to get out the house and to meet other writers who would be participating in workshops that weekend.

Though I didn't get out of the body cast in time for the event, I felt such overwhelming joy to socialize with others that the awkwardness of the cast didn't bother me. Poets are a compassionate crowd, and perhaps they liked me even more for having a story about survival.

On stage that evening, I got a preview of what teaching large crowds of students might feel like. I looked out into the auditorium and quickly blessed each person with love, hoping that I might entertain them or touch their hearts. If that moment was any indicator of my future, I knew teaching would be a breeze if I kept my focus on my audience and not on myself. As I spoke, I forgot that people were looking at me and my cast. Instead, I scanned the room for the eyes that widened or heads that nodded as I talked. I kept talking to the lovely people who seemed open to my message and touched that I had courage to stand in front of everyone, obviously broken in places but beaming with joy.

In college, public speaking terrified me, and I usually downed three or four whiskey shots before participating in a poetry reading or poetry slam. That evening, I felt peaceful and connected to the crowd. If someone didn't appear receptive to my message, I knew that I should not take it personally. The light could work through me to touch those I needed to reach.

After reading my poem and talking briefly about my accident and near-death experience, I saw a few older people in the crowd brush tears from their eyes. I thought about how age often makes people more receptive to discussions about the afterlife. I looked forward to teaching poetry to students of all ages and mixing in metaphysical discussions into lectures. Perhaps my life had been saved so that I might help students, teaching them lessons of openness and love.

At workshops later the next afternoon, I met a couple of poets who told me about a magical sounding place in Helotes called The Home where they met for evening meditations. They promised to swing by and pick me up, so I took them up on this offer the next week. Some evenings at The Home a coyote howled during meditation, and the sounds of nature perfectly augmented those magical moments. The guided meditations were led by a relaxed, charismatic man from California named Charlie. He smoked exactly one cigarette after meditations, claiming that his energy level was so elevated after meditation that one cigarette was about the same as L.A. air.

The meditations proved intense for me, and I often floated somewhere far away from my body, in a beautiful, light-filled place. Meditation allowed me to access the love I felt on the other side, and sometimes tears would stream down my face when I realized the meditation was coming to an end. I felt an ache for the love I experienced in the presence of God.

Sometimes pain prevented me from sitting in the lotus position and I had to recline. Still, I kept visualizing my body healing and opened my heart to all the older people in the crowd who suffered from arthritis, knee surgery, and other ailments. In my suffering, I felt connected to all the others who suffered.

The empty-nest couple who opened their home to everyone were supportive and loving to me. They gave me CDs from Caroline Myss and Deepak Chopra, and when they hugged me for a long while, they felt like my spiritual parents. In my entire life, I had never experienced a place as peaceful as The Home, and I know that peace added healing to my journey.

* * *

During my recovery, I followed Tony Danza's progress because he broke his back during a skiing accident a few months before my accident. I knew Tony Danza would have the best possible rehabilitation facilities at his disposal. He got his body cast off in less than four months, so that was my goal. I also read about back patients who regained muscular strength through water therapy, so I couldn't wait to get out of my body cast and into the water.

A little over four months after my accident, Mom drove me to Austin, and after Doctor Flawn reviewed the X-rays, she called us into her office. Enthusiastically, she pointed to the X-ray and said, "Look at how your bones have regrown around the rods. This is phenomenal progress."

I was thrilled at the thought of getting out of the body cast, and she sent me down the hall to have it sawed off. Getting the cast off this soon meant I could return to classes at U.T. that January. As soon as I got home, I took a shower and that first shower after a Texas summer spent in a body cast felt like heaven. I scrubbed my back for a long while, carefully avoiding the long incision mark that still looked raised, irritated, and very red.

Mom bought comfrey leaves and an aloe vera plant to speed the healing of the scar, and in a few short weeks, the red, irritated scar looked much milder. Jim helped me find a gym conveniently located walking distance from the house. For hours, I simply jogged in the pool, preparing myself for the day I could run again. The angels had promised me that I would run again, and I was counting on it.

Since I was out of the cast, I called some of the poets from the festival and suggested they take me out to hear live music in San Antonio. Everything felt new again, even entering a club. As soon as our small, eclectic group stepped through the door into a crowd bar, the exact guy that I imagined—curly, dark hair, my height, green shirt, and a Walt Whitmanesque hat walked up to me, shook my hand and asked, "Are you from Austin?"

Knowing I was in the middle of the scene I worked on manifesting, I wondered if I should alter the scene or let it play out the way I imagined it. I replied, "I am from Austin, but I had to take a break and live here for a while."

He nodded and said, "You should return soon."

As he walked away, I didn't know what to do. Why didn't I imagine this random stranger handing me a check for a million dollars or something more exciting? Manifesting this moment freaked me out. It took a month to learn how to lucid dream, and it took even longer to manifest this one moment, but I had done it. The power felt challenging and difficult to wield. I knew that I couldn't control everything about my reality and only could control a few trivial things with extreme focus and concentration. Who had the time for the necessary visualization?

Throughout the evening, I felt ecstatic though. I hardly listened to the band, looking around for the guy I manifested, but I never caught sight of him again. Our small group danced near the stage, and I met a guy who was wearing a halo who had fractured his neck the same month that I broke my back. We awkwardly danced together for a moment, laughing at my clunky back brace and his radiating halo. However, we were happy to be alive, despite the hardware holding our bodies together. Everything seemed magical in my world.

CHAPTER TEN

RETURNING TO AUSTIN

"Love is what we were born with.
Fear is what we learned here."
—Marianne Williamson

Before I knew it, the leaves fell from the trees, and we experienced a mild winter, typical of South Texas. Christmas flew by, and I spent pleasant time with Mom and Jim eating healthy food and watching movies. When I registered for classes at U.T., I felt happy to hear the deep voice of William Livingston, the voice of the iconic TEX registration system. His "goodbye and good luck" message seemed to carry me through each semester in some fortunate way. With this return to Austin, I looked forward living a healthier life, studying more, and checking out open-minded churches.

A few days before I left for college, I attended a sweat lodge outside of San Antonio. The shaman's words sounded true, grounded, and deeply connected to the earth. I felt mesmerized by his presence. He told us that women would eventually have greater power in this country and that they should learn from the mistakes of men and not misuse their power. This teaching resonated with me, and I tried to imagine what it would be like to have greater power and influence in the world than my mother or grandmother experienced.

A few days after returning to Austin, I unexpectedly saw Jake walk out of a convenience store. He turned back around as I paid for my Clif bar, placing his hand on the glass outside of the building and looking at me. There was tenderness and sadness in his gaze, and the gesture touched me. He didn't stay to talk with me, and as he walked away, I realized I was much stronger now than I was a year ago. Jake's negative predictions for my future seemed laughable; he certainly didn't imagine that I would meet God and be given a message to teach others. I prayed that he found some grace and healing in his life.

During those first weeks back in Austin, my senses were heightened, and I often knew what someone was going to say ten minutes before they said it. I took a job at a new pizza joint near campus, and these types of psychic flashes happened frequently. For instance, I would get a visual of a man with a long gray beard and large white standard poodle walking by the front door. I would see a vision of myself returning to the kitchen area, and hearing the cook ask me where I grew up. Ten minutes later, the exact scenario I saw play out in my head would happen. After too many of these moments, I prayed that my flashes would come only in the form of a dream, and they slowly faded away.

I picked this humble job because I didn't want to work around the late-night crowds. I worked late afternoon shifts and took morning classes. Before it got dark, I walked home to my room on Fifty-First Street near The Flight Path Coffee House. The women in that rental house were wild and funny.

Sia, a petite, long-haired yoga instructor, who grew bean sprouts on the counter and dated a computer engineer, introduced me to her boyfriend's roommate.

Though I wasn't quite ready to jump into dating, Chip put me at ease with his honesty and analytical mind. Chip also had great legs from riding his bike for hours to combat his hyperactivity, and I found him attractive. However, I decided I should take things slowly, feeling somewhat insecure about my scar and altered, weakened body. I was only a few months out of the back brace.

Sia assured me that Chip was a good catch and made a good living, but I did not care about whatever a good catch meant. I wanted to be loved and understood; getting married had not crossed my mind. When Chip and I talked on the phone, I told him I needed to log seventy-two hours of conversation with him before I would consider having sex with him. I simply made up a number, but he honored it. He kept me on the phone way past my bedtime, talking for two and a half hours that first night. Our dates lingered over dinner, racking up the hours, sometimes going for coffee afterwards and talking, talking, talking late into the night. I had hope for the first time with a man.

Chip's touches and goodnight kisses were sweeter than my somewhat cold, disloyal first boyfriend. Chip also seemed more sensitive than Jake, not the kind of man who would ever tear me to shreds, even if I behaved horribly. He had an emotional strength to his character that I hadn't encountered in anyone before him. We talked about previous relationships, our childhoods, our wildest dreams for the future, and the most embarrassing moments of our lives. We talked about what we wanted from love, where we hoped to travel, and our favorite foods. I panicked at times, fearing that I would be the one to leave him someday, but I didn't tell him this. I hoped the brokenness I felt around romantic relationships might heal by being with him.

Eventually, we made it to the last hours of necessary conversation, and I felt good about making logical decisions about sex, and we even got tested for STDs. When we made love for the first time, I cried with happiness, feeling closer to Chip than I had ever felt to a man. I did not feel the overwhelming sense of desperation and passion that I felt with Jake, but I felt a peaceful, beautiful happiness and satisfaction. Our romance had a feel from another time, not one of nearly instantaneous hookups.

Chip had a way of making me feel safe, as if his very energy drove away men who pursued me or harassed me on the streets. On the way to class, I remember walking on The Drag and an older man came out of bar with slurred speech. He grabbed my arm and aggressively said, "Let me take you out sometime, sexy."

I replied with a bit of force, "I have a boyfriend."

The guy backed away quickly, saying, "Okay, okay. I'm sorry."

Sometimes, it felt strange to be back in Austin—the land where people thought it was normal to drink five-cent beer from seven a.m. to nine a.m. simply because a new restaurant had opened and didn't have a liquor license. Things that appealed to me previously now seemed disgusting. Chip wasn't into drinking and focused more on his health, so I adapted to his ways, feeling healthy and energetic.

As the semester neared completion, the Austin Capitol 10K approached. Nina and several other friends signed up to run the race with me. Chip went out of town for a bike race, and I was happy to spend the weekend with friends who wanted to celebrate this milestone. Several people from my classes stood on the sidelines to cheer for me, and Nina and I jogged behind a large group of military guys. Their chants kept our pace strong for most of the race.

Though that weekend was a lovely marker, I had worries hanging over my head; mainly, money was increasingly becoming an issue. Mom committed herself to paying the lowest possible payments on my hospital bills, even though I assured her that I would file bankruptcy as soon as I could pay a lawyer. Because she continued to do this, she sent me less money. Dad had reached the end of the ten-thousand-dollar loan he took out to help me, though I am certain that he spent a good portion of that loan money on himself. My hospital bills were over one hundred fifty thousand dollars, and I knew I would most likely make less than thirty thousand dollars my first year of teaching at a public school.

I hated to take out more student loans, but I was already working close to thirty-five hours, and the last two classes for my degree plan were tough ones. However, I knew I would pass and graduate because I became a much more persistent student after my near-death experience. After all, no one was going to get in the way of my mission from God. I am sure that I annoyed my linguistics professor with my visits to almost every one of her office hours, but I got the grade I wanted.

Graduation weekend blessed Austin with amazing weather, and Mom, Aunt Heidi, and Dad drove in for the day. We visited a few beautiful locations around town, and my aunt Heidi snapped a picture of Dad and me making the longhorn symbol near the 360 Bridge. The four of us hiked up Mount Bonnell and looked at the view of the city, the water skiers, and all the beautiful homes.

Graduation was a sharp contrast to the previous year when I was forcing myself to walk for the first time in the hospital, crying as I looked out the hospital window at the U.T. tower. Now, I was a part of that huge, celebratory crowd. Dan Rather spoke to us, and Cindy and I took swigs from a bottle of champagne she smuggled in under her gown. At some point, I turned around, wondering if I could see Breckinridge Hospital from the quad. I couldn't, but I felt an enormous amount of joy just to be alive and able to walk.

Graduation was an emotional milestone, but I had to wait until fall semester to take the classes needed for a teaching certification. I felt uncertain about what to do with myself over the summer. Chip and I had only been dating a few months, so I felt uncomfortable bringing up the idea of moving in with him. I also did not want to return to Mom's house for the summer. I liked the freedom of being on my own. On a whim, I saw an ad in the *Austin Chronicle* for a dog-watcher for two elderly golden retrievers and part-time maid/server in Maine.

Though I did not last long working for the bitter matriarch of the Hargrave family, I felt grateful to be out of Texas for a month and half, and when I quit the job, Chip spontaneously met me in Maine for a free-spirited vacation. One of the happiest moments of my life occurred on that trip.

After a few nights in Bar Harbor, we headed up the coast to Arcadia National Park. I had never hiked a particularly large mountain, so we started out on easy to moderate hikes. Eventually, I got the courage to try Beehive Trail, not realizing it would be a particularly windy day and we would have to climb straight up holding on to metal spokes nailed into the mountain. My limbs shook with exhaustion because we had hiked another mountain that morning.

Chip was not winded, but he patiently waited for me to make it to the top, and the view was spectacular. We could see the ocean and the rocky coast from this vantage point. Since I was hungry, I wanted to immediately climb back down the mountain; however, when I walked a few steps I became shaky, dizzy, and tired. In a hypoglycemic haze, I wondered out loud how I would make it down the mountain. Chip convinced me to rest while he jogged back down the mountain to get power bars.

I argued for a moment until I realized that I needed his help. Climbing those two mountains had taken everything I had, and I smiled as I watched him take off like a sure-footed deer down the trails. While he was gone, I rested on the sun-baked rocks and took long, deep breaths, feeling the presence of the divine come to me and filling me with peace. I felt happy looking at this beautiful world of ours and blessed to have a sweet boyfriend willing to serve me in that way. I had everything in that moment—an amazing view, a connection to God, a connection to nature, and a great love.

What more could a young woman want? I didn't need the Hargrave's twelve thousand square foot summer home because I had Beehive and a view much lovelier than those unhappy, vengeful millionaires. I didn't need their five-star chef because I had someone who loved me enough to jog up a mountain just to bring me food. My life shimmered with joy, and I felt blessed simply to breathe.

CHAPTER ELEVEN

STUDENT TEACHING ASSIGNMENT

"Sometimes people think compassion is only of help to others, while we get no benefit. This is a mistake. When you concern yourself with others, you naturally develop a sense of self-confidence. To help others takes courage and inner strength."
—Dalai Lama

Back in Austin, I felt a new certainty; the certainty that came with knowing that more people needed to experience unconditional love. Though this unconditional love could be practiced in everyday life situations, I felt excited to have an audience of students. I would do my best to love them all, and God's love would be my model and guiding principle. I felt a growing anxiousness to follow my afterlife mission and get into a classroom.

While I was taking the classes required for a teaching certification, I met new idealistic friends who also wanted to make a difference in the lives of the youth of America. To many of us, school had brought more order, knowledge, love, and understanding into our lives, even if this grace had come from only one teacher who had shown us how to believe in ourselves. We all wanted to be that teacher who might give confidence to someone in need of support.

Though I met many wonderful classmates, Grayson became my closest friend because of his interest in poetry, travel, and spirituality. We shared poems and talked about all the places we wanted to visit around the world. One afternoon at a café overlooking a crowded Austin sidewalk, Grayson asked me if I still saw angels or received messages from them. His question hurt me because I didn't see angels anymore, and I realized how much I longed for this connection.

When I looked up from the salad I was eating, I instantly saw hundreds of angels all around the café and surrounding the people on the sidewalk. The image disappeared as quickly as it showed up, and I excused myself to go to the restroom to compose myself. I felt shocked by the beauty of the moment and missed the other side. Even if we aren't aware of angels, I knew they were there for us.

When I went back to the table, Grayson shared some of his channeled poetry and automatic writing; I smiled, happy to listen. Grayson proved a fantastic addition to my small group of spiritual friends. Nina and her roommate, Clyde, were two of my closest friends, and my life outside of classes mainly consisted of walking around Town Lake, doing yoga, eating healthy meals, going to New Age bookstores, and attending musical festivals. The hungover, highly depressed young woman from my past had mostly disappeared. When I saw young people around campus who reminded me of my former self, I smiled at them, hoping some of my good energy might change their outlook.

As I followed orders and worked toward a career in education, my whole being felt flooded with energy. How could I not be excited about a mission from God? I walked the streets of Austin, feeling connected to everyone, behaving much like a happy child, floating in a bubble of peacefulness. Austin is a happy, youth-infused, carefree city, and I felt buoyant as I walked through crowds. Often, I started random conversations with people at checkout counters, listening to stories about their lives and offering advice.

My steps were light and free, and I walked through campus smiling widely and probably a bit idiotically. I couldn't stop grinning at everyone who passed by me, and it's possible to pass by a lot of people in Austin. Students were often busy and focused. Many people smiled or nodded back, but people in the downtown area on their way to work often looked annoyed by my joyfulness. I saw frustration and disappointment in many people, and I longed to remind them of their connection to the love of God.

This oneness with everyone was both amazing and annoying. Sometimes, I picked up on things that people felt guilty about, and I wanted to remind them to focus on love. Since I had merged with everyone's consciousness in Austin during my near-death experience, I wondered if the feelings of oneness were especially powerful for me while in Austin. Whatever the case, I felt overjoyed simply to be alive and to have any role on Earth, and I saw the light of God in everyone whom I encountered.

* * *

For my student teaching assignment, I worked with a supervising teacher at Stephen F. Austin High, a cool location for a high school near Town Lake. Though I heard horror stories about supervising teachers, I hoped that my supervisor would love her profession and be a good mentor to me.

After greeting me, my supervising teacher, Missus Rutherford, looked me over and shuffled toward a large file cabinet in her long floral dress that hung tent-like over her apple shaped figure. After she gave me a spiel that I'm sure she gave to countless other student teachers, she ended with this bit of advice, "Don't bother trying to reach students like T.J. He's a druggie, a thug, and he'll drop out soon enough."

I told Missus Rutherford, "I'll do my best with the classes. I'm here to connect with the students in my way. I want to reach the lost and broken students of the world. That's why I'm here."

Her demeanor immediately changed, and I realized that no matter what kind of magic I worked in the classroom, she would never give me the highest score on my review. Missus Rutherford shuffled from foot to foot in her comfortable loafers, one of which often seemed to be untied, and said, "You should move to a city like Portland, Oregon. Or maybe Seattle, Washington. So that way you can be all touchy feely." She paused before continuing, "This is not an easy group of students. My bet is that you'll be begging me to come in and create order in two days. They'll run over you."

Missus Rutherford gave me her least favorite classes and probably accepted the role of supervising teacher not to help new teachers succeed but to get out of teaching herself. I didn't care. *The less interference from her, the better,* I thought. I blessed her and hoped I never became as tired and disillusioned with my profession as she clearly was with hers.

From the first moment in the classroom, I opened myself to the possibility of having angels work through me. As soon as Missus Rutherford stepped out of the classroom, and I was alone with my students, I asked them to introduce each other with a fun fact, figuring that they deserved a break after putting up with Missus Rutherford for a semester.

My group of high school juniors were exactly what one might expect from an Austin group. Most were worldly and tolerant; some were foreign exchange students with a certain level of maturity. Some of the guys wore their hair a bit longer. Some of the young women were thoughtful and shy; others were flirtatious and boy crazy. A few had come out. Many of the students were readers, thinkers, and curious about me. A few were bored with high school and didn't give a crap about me. A few students were sheltered and possibly moved to Austin from the country. I loved them all immediately and felt privileged to be in their lives. I believed that my unconditional love, much like the unconditional love of the divine, would be the key to connecting with them. I gave my heart and soul to those students, trusting that even the toughest ones might be influenced by what I had to say, even if I didn't see the results in my time with them.

I started with a lesson on Walt Whitman because it gave me a chance to talk about my near-death experience. I'd never told a group of students my full story, but I decided to see how they might react. I wove the story in to the ending of *Leaves of Grass* where Whitman talks about departing as air and drifting in "lacy jags."

I was honest with the students, and told them who how I had lived my life before my afterlife experience. Certainly, they were familiar with the undergraduates who puked their guts out on Sixth Street, occasionally even smoking pot in public. I told them about my childhood and how I had turned away from religion because I was angry at the authority figures in my life. I shared with them how I was so surprised that consciousness goes on after death.

They let me speak and listened as I told them my full near-death experience story. To my surprise and delight, they hardly blinked or averted their eyes from me. No one whispered, no one took a restroom break, and no one even checked the clock. Even T.J., the student Missus Rutherford had warned me about, stopped his frantic pen tapping and put his head down on the desk, sometimes looking up at me with wary curiosity. When I looked at him, I emphasized my drug and alcohol use and how much better I felt, clear-headed and recovering at my Mom's house.

The students asked me several questions about the angels and if I thought I would like teaching. We talked informally in the few minutes remaining before the bell, and several students hung around after the bell, not wanting to go to their next class.

A student named Clarence who sat in the front row felt like an ally from the first day; he stayed behind and asked if he could talk to me. Clarence seemed wise beyond his years. That day, he told me that he was nineteen years old and had been out of school for a couple of years because of a brain injury and coma. He, too, had experienced a near-death experience, but he had not told anyone about his experience. He seemed relieved to talk openly with me, and I told him to write about his experience during journal time. I would comment on his thoughts and allow him to process the experience. Clarence seemed mature, and I imagined professors felt connections like this with some of their students.

T.J., however, kept me grounded firmly in what it is like to teach high school students. His resistance to the classroom proved intense. Occasionally, he came in with red eyes, addled and completely out of it. Though I was familiar with some drugs, I wasn't sure what he took. Some afternoons, T.J. walked on the chairs and tables, and I had to pull his desk outside the classroom and tell him to stay in the hall.

One afternoon, when I talked with the principal, I suggested an alternative school for T.J. He smirked and said, "There isn't room in the alternative school, or in detention. You're going to have to deal with T.J. yourself."

My jaw dropped, and I didn't have a reply. I gathered my things and walked out of his office, never to interact with him again. This might've been an initiation of sorts, but I didn't appreciate the lack of support.

Obviously, I had to do something about T.J. I prayed for a breakthrough with him, and that breakthrough eventually happened one afternoon while riding the city bus home with T.J. and one of his friends. He was studying for a history test, and his buddy was making fun of him because he didn't know the difference between the nations and leaders during WWI and WWII. T.J. thought WWI started because of Hitler.

I stepped in and helped them both study. I found out that T.J.'s brother was in a gang, and he became a part of it as well, somewhat by default. He felt he never had a chance in school. I asked him if he planned to drop out, and he nodded. For a while, I simply observed him, and he seemed sober that day. This made him seem innocent, skinny, and young, especially while sitting in the middle of all the older people riding the city bus.

I felt prompted to give him some advice before my stop. Hoping that my angels might talk through me, I told him that if he dropped out a GED would be possible, and that Austin Community College or even a community college in a different town would be a wonderful place to start a new life. We talked about things he enjoyed, like working on cars, and I suggested that a career as a mechanic could help him find a more peaceful life.

I talked with him about positive mindsets and goal-setting: I showed him a few memorization tricks to help study for that history test. I told T.J. again how much better my head felt and how much clearer I thought now that I didn't do drugs. He looked at me thoughtfully, probably more moved by the fact that I cared about him, than by what I said.

By some miracle of God—or through cheating—T.J. got a 73 percent on that test, and he attributed it to my help and let me know. With one moment of success, I didn't want him to give up the momentum, so I made him promise to write the next paper for my English class.

He hadn't written a single paper for Missus Rutherford. His grade was a zero which became an automatic 50 percent. Amazingly, T.J. wrote an essay for me, and it was one of the more creative papers I've received in my many years of teaching. Though his grammar wasn't perfect, the story taught me something about his life. He rewrote John Updike's *A&P* using gang lingo. He created a character like Sammy who chose to stand up and defend the honor of a few good-looking women who were disrespected by a gas station clerk. I loved his remix of the story and felt like this had to be one of my best moments with that group.

T.J. didn't do every assignment after that, but he participated, and I never had to send him out of the room again. I had won some of his respect by talking with him outside of class, but he still came in stoned after lunch many days, and so did a lot of the other students.

One afternoon, when the classroom reeked of pot, I told the students that I knew when they were stoned and that I would appreciate it if they would abstain. I brought in studies which demonstrated how much better the brain works and retains information when sober. We talked about health, mental health, and depression. They were more receptive than I imagined they might be and tried the mindfulness exercises I suggested.

They listened when I told them how I used my mind to overcome pain after my accident. A few students stayed after class and said they were interested in these topics and hoped to study psychology in college. Amazingly, they stayed sober for most of that semester, or simply hid the smell of pot better. Whatever the case, I felt closer to them.

* * *

Though I loved working with the students, the long hours took a lot out of me. Since I didn't have a car, I woke up at five a.m. each morning and rode the bus to Stephen F. Austin High. Many times, I didn't get home until after six p.m., and I still had paperwork. I could only work a few shifts on the weekend and relied heavily on student loans.

Chip, who had boundless energy, often stayed up late working on the creation of an action adventure video game at Go-Go Studios. Often, I envied his ADHD for all the energy he seemed to have for accomplishing things late into the night and then later riding his bike for several hours a day.

I loved him, but sometimes he annoyed me, interrupting my lesson planning by bringing me random gifts like the plastic stopper on a grocery cart that could've been peed on by a homeless person. I didn't understand why he didn't bring me a cup of coffee, a smoothie, or anything helpful. After a few more irritating interactions with Chip, I told him that I wanted a break.

I also felt flares of jealousy about one of the designers on his team. I thought she might be a better match for him—someone with his same interest in video games. She seemed intellectually compatible with him and had a certain laid-back style that I envied, especially now that I spent a lot of time dressing the part of a teacher in long, frumpy dresses. I didn't know how to fully communicate my insecurities to Chip. He assured me that nothing was going on with her, but his lack of tact irritated me when he said, "She's really attractive, but I let my friend ask her out since we're dating."

Since I didn't have the mental space to worry much about my decision to break up with him, I pushed the thought of a relationship out of mind and concentrated on teaching. U.T. required us to check back in at the campus for a few days mid-semester, so I returned to campus for a few days. When I returned, Missus Rutherford was in a great mood and couldn't wait to tell me what had happened while I was gone. When she passed back the papers I graded, Christina, a petite, spunky girl, called me a "fucking bitch" because she didn't like her grade. T.J. decided to defend my honor by saying, "Miss Barker isn't a bitch, but you are a stupid fucking cunt who needs to shut the fuck up."

I reached T.J., but the results were not exactly what I hoped for. Both students were sent to detention for a week, and Missus Rutherford couldn't stop talking about that day. She found it highly amusing, and I wondered if she had egged on the conflict. I knew I could've handled that moment differently.

Christina returned a week later with her head down, avoiding my curious gaze. T.J. dropped out, and I never saw him again. I kept Christina after class and asked her what grade she wanted in the class. She said she wanted an A, but she'd be fine with a B. We looked at her paper, and I showed her how to structure it and how to rewrite it to make it stronger. While working with Christina, I realized that some of the students who called me a bitch in one moment might grow to like me later.

Christina was hurting and wanted to be successful in school. I showed her how to be a better writer, and I showered her with compliments. Her attitude improved even more than her writing. Christina gave me respect, and we got along without any trouble for the rest of that semester. She even ended up with a high B in the class and earned it.

My German foreign exchange student shared her poetry with me, and like Clarence, she felt more like a friend than a student. I was sad to see the semester end and told them so. They, of course, told me that I was a better teacher than Missus Rutherford and that they were excited for my future students.

Missus Rutherford gave me mostly threes on my review, and a four only on a section about student engagement. A four is the highest mark, and even Missus Rutherford couldn't deny that the students paid attention and certainly tried much harder in my class than they had in her class.

The week before I took the state exam to officially become a teacher, Nina and Clyde took me to First Spiritualist Church of Austin where members of the audience could practice their intuitive gifts. Though the frequency of my psychic flashes had slowed down after I prayed to receive messages only through dreams, I couldn't help being curious about people who embraced their gifts.

Clyde embraced the New Age community fully, getting certified in Reiki and several other healing arts. Nina poked fun of him, saying he gave better readings and more energy to cuter guys who came to him for advice. A couple of the guys in that class of high school juniors had flirted with me, but I felt a certain purity about my profession. I considered it a blessing if students liked me because I would never cross any inappropriate boundaries. Instead, I would only have a better chance of saying something that mattered to them if I held their attention through a crush. My students' souls were in my care, and I wanted those hours to be about their mental, spiritual, and emotional growth. The classroom was my sanctuary.

Maybe some spiritual leaders can't keep the appropriate distance between themselves and clients, thus allowing sexual attraction to taint the experience. I've heard people talk of gurus manifesting and de-manifesting around sexual issues. Though I was clear about my role in the classroom, relationships outside of the classroom didn't seem to be enveloped in the same divine light. I had trouble staying in a relationship, even with someone as smart and sweet as Chip.

When I met a couple at the First Spiritualist Church of Austin who seemed unbelievably in love, I asked them their secret. A light glowed around the two of them, and if I had ever seen two people who were soul mates, I felt certain these two were it. They smiled and said people often asked them this question.

Like Chip and me, they had waited a long while before ever kissing or becoming intimate. They knew from the first meeting that they were attracted to each other, but they both had wounds from their past and unresolved issues from childhood and didn't feel ready for a relationship. They made a vow to talk for an entire year before kissing.

I wondered if my seventy-two hours of conversation with Chip had not been enough to forge a solid relationship. Our emotional closeness made our relationship the healthiest one of my life, but it hadn't brought us to the same place as this couple. On an emotional and spiritual level, their process sounded amazing. They pulled two couches into her living room, and they slept on separate couches, talking late into the night and deeply listening to one another. Much of what counselors get paid to do is to deeply listen, so I can imagine that listening brought them both peace and healing. She said that she knew almost every one of his childhood wounds, romantic wounds, his wishes, his dreams, and desires by the end of that year. He also understood her fears, wounds, desires, and hopes.

I asked if it was difficult not to kiss, and they both laughed, saying they also got that question a lot. She said that they felt completely one before they ever kissed, often dreaming of each other and feeling each other's presence long before the consummation of those desires. I thought about how even at a young age, many of us have so many wounds. Most people don't take the time to get to know one another deeply before becoming intimate. Intimacy opens all the wounds and then people end up getting triggered and terrified when all they needed was more understanding and compassion.

Though this sounded like a logical and wonderful plan, I wondered out loud if I could be as strong. On the drive back home, Nina and Clyde told me to shut up about the couple and get back together with Chip since I obviously missed him. I called him that night and he rushed to me. It felt amazing to reconnect, but I realized how badly I had hurt him.

A large part of my heart hoped that I could remain with him this time, forging a solid, long-term relationship. Another part of me longed for adventure in the form of something I couldn't even put into words—wild, random nights in foreign countries, meeting strangers and kissing outside near a fountain, conversations about novelists and philosophers in a moonlit cafe, stealing dragon-shaped paddleboats and paddling out into the middle of a lake, jumping off cliffs and swimming far into the ocean.

Chip seemed more whole than me, more real when it came to romance. I didn't understand why I could disconnect easily from my feelings, but I could, possibly because of the emotional and physical abuse I suffered as a child. I didn't bother trying to fully trust or love anyone after Jake because I feared another loss like that might kill me. I didn't know what I wanted from relationships, but a part of me loved to run away from love—fast—into a new reality before love imploded. I also wondered if the near-death experience made me feel unconditional love for most people and unable to fully concentrate my energy on one person. Still, I held onto the image of the soul mate couple, hoping they were as in love and happy as they appeared. Though romantic love presented challenges for me, I committed fully to what I knew would always be a part of life: change.

* * *

I passed the state exams and applied for a few teaching jobs in Austin, but nothing panned out. Chip and I wanted to live somewhere other than Texas, so we hit the road for an adventurous road trip, checking out places we might want to live. Though fun, the road trip cut into time I might have spent looking for a job, but I trusted that everything would work out. I had applied for a couple of positions overseas, and Chip felt somewhat open to the possibility of following me overseas.

On the drive north, we stopped in East Texas to see my dad, and my grandmother who had Alzheimer's. After one or two loops through the few stories that she remembered, I grabbed her hand, suddenly sensing this might be the last time I would see my grandmother alive. I connected with a light in her eyes and saw that she was getting closer to that light. I wondered if I could sense when people were close to dying.

For a split second, she became lucid as I held her hand. My grandmother knew nothing about Chip because I told my dad very little about my life. Suddenly, like her former animated self, she looked at Chip and said, "Do you work with computers?"

He smiled, and said, "Yes, I'm a programmer."

She hit the sides of her wheelchair and looked at me and said, "Oh my heavens, you better hang on to this one, Tricia. He's a good catch. Will you please marry him?"

Grandmother, a religious woman, loved me dearly and wanted the best for me. It touched me that she had a lucid moment and realized that Chip was a good guy.

As we drove out of East Texas, I felt sad, wishing I spent more time with Grandmother Clara while I was growing up. I had precious few memories of her, but I knew her love for me was strong. My grandmother's love felt light and joyous, and I couldn't believe that a few brief moments were all we had in this life. When she reached the other side, I knew she would see how much love I had in my heart for her.

Chip and I hiked in the humid Arkansas forests, and then drove straight through to Chicago. Once there, I gave Chip time to hang out with his friend and checked out a poetry reading. Dave, a nerdy looking guy who ran the open mike, introduced himself and said he produced a literary magazine.

He wanted to feature my work, so I gave him a copy of a publication that had recently published one of my poems and said he could use that poem along with the picture. I jotted down my parent's address and number, so that he could send me his publication and didn't think much more of the moment.

Chip and I continued to Thunder Bay, and I fell in love with Canada in the summer. We camped out a lot and watched the northern lights from our tent. Though we lived in a somewhat free-spirited way, I was worried about September and where I might get a job. At this point, I realized that I might have to substitute teach for a year before I could get into a school district or graduate school.

Chip was less concerned about money and said I didn't have to worry about finances because he received monthly checks from two well-known video games that he worked on right out of college. However, stress about my future weighed heavily on my mind. While in Austin, I had a flash that I would be on a plane to South Korea or Japan shortly, and I couldn't get this image out of my head.

After camping in Canada, I stopped enjoying all the many beautiful sights because of my growing anxiety. I cried late into the night, sometimes thinking about my childhood and feeling a deep loneliness and longing. Chip wanted to have kids, but I never wanted to have them if that meant leaving them with my mother for any unsupervised time. I also never wanted to turn into someone like her. To me, the decision to not have kids seemed a simple solution. This decision depressed me, but all I knew is that I had to teach. God didn't give me a mission to come back and have kids.

When we arrived at Chip's sister's house outside of Boston, I considered the possibility a job in South Korea seriously. I had not been called back by any of the school districts I applied to in Austin and Portland. One morning while making omelets, Chip asked me to pass the salsa and said, "I'm thinking of something and it begins with the letter *m*.

I knew exactly what he meant, but the romantic part of me was disgusted by his roundabout way of discussing marriage. If he really wanted to marry me, I needed something more concrete like a big-ass ring, a high-quality restaurant, a plan to help me deal with my student loans, a decision about where we might live, and how we might work international travel into our lives. I needed reassurance that I could find a good teaching position the next year. I needed confidence, a damned good proposal, and a lot of reassurance, not the letter *m*.

I sighed and said, "That was the worst proposal ever. You can't actually think you are ready for marriage if you can't even say the damn word."

I wasn't ready for marriage, and I left him a few days later. He threw my clothes off the balcony and then immediately came down the stairs and helped me pick them up and hugged me for a long while. We cried together, and I hoped I wasn't making a mistake.

A few weeks later, I was on a plane to South Korea.

PART II

CHAPTER TWELVE

SOUTH KOREA

"A mind that is stretched
by a new experience can never go
back to its old dimensions."
—Oliver Wendell Holmes, Jr.

I looked out the window as the airplane descended closer to the mountains of South Korea, and temple rooftops jutted out of pink clouds of sunrise. The beauty of these rocky mountaintop refuges beckoned me, and I wondered what new perspectives living in Korea would bring. I imagined spending my free time meditating in temples and appreciating life with greater mindfulness. I wasn't prepared for the noise pollution, the venders selling hot chestnuts through megaphones at five in the morning, and the constant stream of cars.

After a few weeks of getting settled into an apartment on the twenty-fourth floor of a poured concrete building that I shared with two other English teachers from California, a group of South Korean teachers invited the new teachers for a trip to Yosu. My roommate, Jackson, declined, but my other roommate, Rachel, and her Canadian boyfriend joined the group. On that trip, I quickly learned that Rachel didn't care much for other women. She told me that she was raised by her father while her mother was absent. I couldn't help hoping that she would warm up to me and see me as a caring female friend.

In Yosu we were told to get up very early. By four a.m., our Korean tour guides guided us up a steep mountain; we shivered and followed their line of flashlights. Eventually, we made it to the top. In darkness, punctuated only by candlelight and the red tips of incense, we sat cross-legged on a big marble floor and listened to monks chanting; soon, the sun rose over the ocean, and blazing golden light poured through the temple. The huge golden Buddha and the many small, golden statues glistened beautifully. The trip to Yosu made my decision to come to South Korea seem perfect. I considered writing to *Lonely Planet*, one of my favorite travel guides, to tell them about this spot in Yosu but decided to keep the beautiful experience to myself.

Back in town, the workweeks were long and demanding. I taught students of all ages—college students in the morning, preschoolers in the early afternoon, and elementary, junior high, high school, and adults until late at night. My students were pleasant—respectful, kind, and curious. Even the junior high kids were well-behaved, though a bit goofy as junior high kids tend to be in any culture, often teasing one another relentlessly. One afternoon, I asked the junior high class to teach me the Korean word for "shut up," and they told me it was "penis." You can imagine the horror of the Korean English teachers as I yelled, "Penis!" very loudly.

Korean teachers encouraged us to spend time with the students outside of class, and the parents welcomed any opportunity for the students to keep practicing conversational English. Many kind parents invited me to dinner at their house or brought me dinner while I worked at the Hagwan. I heard stories about how most American parents complained to teachers or emailed them about issues, so I soaked up the love and attention from all the Kunsan parents.

I remember noticing the junior high student's obsession with video games and technology. Years later, when I heard about Koreans who died in these video bongs (large rooms full of computers where many teenagers and young adults stayed up all night playing games) because they didn't even get up to go to the restroom while playing these games, I hoped that none of my students met with that fate.

After a few months in town, I wanted to do something special for my wild junior high group; I asked them if they wanted to go for an outing, and they picked a location to play video games. Though I wasn't interested in games, I asked the students what they enjoyed about the experience. These boisterous, funny kids had worked their way into my heart.

Working professionals took my latest class which lasted from nine p.m. to ten p.m. Our discussions covered current business trends, politics, travel, college, food, family life, and friendships. Mostly, these students were tired after a long day of work, but they wanted to move up in their companies and believed that conversational English would help them. A few men didn't take the classes seriously, showed up drunk, and asked me pointed, intimate questions.

Because English teachers were advertised in the newspapers with our pictures and degrees, many taxi drivers in town knew my name the minute they saw me. Most English teachers felt like minor celebrities. When the taxi drivers picked up me and my two roommates they were overjoyed to see all three of us at one time and pointed at each of us, saying our names.

After less than a month of being in town, I took a break between my classes and stood on the corner of our Hagwan's street drinking a coffee and looking at the crowded streets. The long days of teaching were wearing on me, so I thought a cigarette might give me energy to make it until ten o'clock. I was wearing sunglasses, which I didn't think anything of at the time, when out of nowhere a drunk man jumped out of a taxi, ran across the street, bought a dozen roses and thrust them at me. He grabbed my arm and pulled me toward the taxi, saying in loud English, "We go now. We have sexual intercourse."

I dropped the roses and ran as fast as I could into the Hagwan, but he followed me up the stairs. This red-eyed man, reeking of whiskey, rushed into the lobby where the three young Korean English teachers asked him what he wanted. They laughed and screamed, at him, "No, she's not a prostitute. She's a teacher. A teacher!"

Somehow cigarettes and "mistaken for prostitute" comingled in my mind, and I quit that occasional habit permanently. I also stopped wearing sunglasses and squinted a lot more. I would rather not fend off the advances of drunken, porn-addled men in a country where I only knew enough Korean to buy vegetables in the market and take a taxi.

That evening, my roommates had a good laugh about my story. As we shared takeout Bibimbap, we talked about the many strange stories we were collecting. Apparently, the adults in both Jackson's and Rachel's classes frequently mentioned the bathhouses and invited them to join them. We howled with laughter thinking about how the Koreans longed to see Americans naked.

Though I laughed about the moment with the drunk man, it troubled me some. What if he had pulled me into that taxi? Still, I didn't want fear to limit my freedom. I enjoyed walking around Kunsan and deeply experiencing moments in a foreign country. Sometimes, while receiving change from a sweet young bank teller, I would feel a sudden oneness with everyone in the building and on the streets. A light, feather-like blessing would enter my body, and I felt as if I were floating. With deep sweetness, my soul seemed connected to every soul surrounding me. These moments lasted for a minute or so, but I wanted to get stuck this way. To float through life with this sense of loving connection seemed the ultimate way to live. Other times, I might feel a certain peace that seemed to come from the deep concern and reverence that a waiter might pay me. I felt like royalty as sweet, very young children bowed to me.

During my teaching breaks, I explored the restaurants and stores around the school, sampling unusual chips, cookies, and candies. Shrimp-flavored chips and bubble tea in a can were my favorite treats. For lunch, I searched out very small restaurants and ordered a big spread of food, all under five dollars. Some afternoons, I felt like a queen. I loved being alone with my thoughts, strolling through town, and discovering something new each day.

Kunsan is considered a rural, farming area—even with the two million residents. While walking on the sidewalks, pedestrians had to be prepared for the occasional car that would momentarily jump up on the edge of the sidewalk to avoid a collision. Locals joked that it was easy to get run over by a taxi or bus, and a few taxis brushed so close to my thighs that I had to enter the first store I could find just to catch my breath from the near miss.

One evening outside of our Hagwan, I watched a kindergarten boy from a neighboring school cross the street, most likely headed to one of the convenience stores for a snack. Before he made it to the store, a taxi, which seemed to come out of nowhere, hit him hard. His body broke like a twig. My reality ripped into pieces, and I ran to him, hoping I could comfort him or send him healing energy.

However, the moment I grabbed his little hand, I knew his spirit had already gone from his body and was hovering a few hundred feet away, watching the scene. I kept holding his hand and looked in the direction where I felt he was and sent him love. For a split second, I felt the portal open, and I felt light and love coming for this beautiful little boy.

My vision quickly ended when a random man picked the boy up and ran in the direction of the nearest hospital. I stayed kneeling on the asphalt, holding the one tiny shoe he left behind. The darkness of the evening enveloped me, and I mourned openly, thinking about the sadness his mother would feel as she reached for the phone that afternoon. I could see her deep sorrow and feel her body heaving as she leaned into her husband's embrace. The loss of this beautiful child would be a permanent marker in her heart.

Koreans who had not seen the accident walked past me hurriedly, a strange sight simply because of my long, blonde hair but now all the stranger for my public display of shock. I cried for my own body and the trauma of my wreck. I remembered how close I came to death. I cried for the life this child would not live, but I knew that he would immediately be wrapped in safety and love. I hoped his parents might find peace eventually. I asked around, hoping to be able to contact his parents, but the teachers at my Hagwan didn't know the kid.

For the next few weeks, I thought about how easily our lives can be eradicated like we are little ants swept away by the randomness of events. I continued to pray for his mother and father in the Kunsan temple, bowing several times as I observed others doing. Many of my high school and college students were Christians and thought the temples were for old people, but I loved the smell of the incense and the highly-polished floors. The temples were the only quiet, clean places in town, so I spent hours meditating, focusing on my breathing and letting go of thoughts. Usually, when I opened my eyes, Buddha filled up my vision, and he comforted me, seeming to contain both sadness and joy at the same time.

When the leaves began to change, a beautiful sight in South Korea, homesickness set in, and I longed to return to the States. Most of my dreams were of a quiet backyard, birds chirping in the trees, squirrels squawking at a dog below. Then, I would wake up in my brightly lit apartment with the loud, jarring sounds of traffic and vendors. It would take hours to adjust my consciousness to the idea that I lived in South Korea as the imagined reality didn't live up to the reality of living in South Korea.

Weekend travel continued to be a source of pleasure. My best friend, Kwang Min, drove us through the brightest foliage I had ever witnessed. Tourists were out by the millions, and though the traffic and pollution could be overwhelming, the national parks were beautiful. One of my happiest trips was to Seoraksan National Park with a beautiful Buddhist temple called Sinheungsa Temple. We spent hours walking through the sites and hiking trails. Several curious hikers handed me pears and oranges, and Kwang Min laughed at the celebrity worship of my blonde hair.

Young men stopped to tell me that I looked like Sharon Stone or Gwen Stefani, and Kwang Min rolled her eyes at them. After her ugly divorce, where the court system gave full custody of her two boys to her violent ex-husband, she was done with Korean men. Apparently, divorced women were looked down on in that society, so all her friends were foreigners—mainly teachers and military personnel.

On the weekends, various groups of teachers and a few Korean friends often hopped a bus to Seoul and visited museums, tea houses, and walked along Deoksugung Stone-wall Road—a beautiful place to take in the fall colors. On one bus trip home from Seoul, the roads became icy and a four-hour trip turned into a twelve-hour ordeal. I had never observed traffic jams in the U.S. anything like the ones in South Korea.

While living in Kunsan, most of my interactions with men were innocent and somewhat amusing. I had a crush on a tall, handsome college student who worked at a rose stand near my apartment and played "Tears in Heaven" on his guitar. Unfortunately, he didn't speak English beyond the words of that song. I met him at his sister's house, and every day after that he handed me a rose. His sister, an English teacher at another school, wanted me to date her older brother, a typical conservative engineer. I insisted that I wanted "younger brother" not "older brother."

She always joked and said, "No, no. Older brother is the one for you."

The Koreans felt a certain desperation to marry me off when they found out I was twenty-four. I imagined marrying once I got closer to thirty and considered my twenties a time when I should live an adventurous life. I talked with my high school girls about cultural differences and how many women in U.S. postponed marriage. The high school girls may have listened to me because I kept in touch with a few who ended up at various universities in the U.S.

A few weeks before Christmas, I received a big box at my apartment. I tore into it, hoping Mom sent me vitamins and snacks from the U.S. The novelty of Korean food had worn off. When I opened the box, my heart sank with disappointment because all that I saw was poetry and pictures. Dave, the guy with the literary magazine in Chicago, must've called my parents to get my address in Korea. We talked once at my parents' house before I went to Korea, and he seemed like a fragile narcissist who thought of himself as a poet too great to bother going to college.

I thought that made him sound like an idiot, and I hoped he would forget about sending me his "literary magazine." The box contained hundreds of poems, mostly about oral sex and dedicated to me. I imagined that he simply typed various women's names in the dedication line, hoping this might work on someone.

Disgust turned to horror when I looked through the pictures and saw that Dave had blown up my photo from the magazine and taken blurry doubles of all the places he had put my picture around his house. I was in a frame next to a picture of his mother. He placed a picture of me next to his cats, on his refrigerator, and in his bedroom. The picture in his bedroom was very large. Photoshopping technology was limited in the mid-'90s, so he manually cut out pictures of us and glued them together. One picture featured a giant framed photo of himself with a small picture of me on his shoulder. The caption read, "Who is this angel on my shoulder?"

Disgusted by the package, I quickly wrote a letter and sent it via express mail, telling him never to contact me again. Something was seriously not right with this man. Quickly,

I received a postcard from him and let me know that his romantic nature was often "misunderstood" by women. In this postcard, he wrote that four women had restraining orders placed on him in the past couple of years, including two ex-girlfriends. I wondered if this was his way of warning me that he wouldn't let this go. In the postcard, he referred to himself again as the "greatest poet of all times," and he felt sorry for me that I couldn't grasp how amazing he was and couldn't receive his love.

I burned some of Dave's poems and pictures in the dumpster near my apartment and wondered if I should have taken pictures of the sick mess in case he ever contacted me again, which he did a few times. Luckily, the postcard he sent said that his friends talked him out of coming to South Korea to surprise me. To this day, I feel gratitude when I think of the men who talked Dave out of a trip to South Korea. As bystanders offering some sanity, they made my life easier.

Still, I felt wary and on edge after receiving that package. I couldn't help feeling like a bug under glass. The darkness and unexpected nature of the event troubled me. I couldn't find an answer to why women were often treated as objects both in the U.S. and in Asia. I knew that I was an eternal being, far greater and vaster than my physical form, but being in the body of a young woman was beginning to make my journey feel treacherous.

CHAPTER THIRTEEN

TRAUMA

"You may encounter many defeats,
but you must not be defeated. In fact,
it may be necessary to encounter the defeats, so
you can know who you are, what you can rise
from, how you can still come out of it."
—Maya Angelou

A few days before Christmas Day, which isn't widely celebrated in South Korea, the weather changed, and we had our first snow. We didn't have many snowy Christmases in Texas, so I took pictures and reveled in sweet moments with my elementary kids as we threw snowballs at each other. During the holiday season, the American, British, Canadian, and Australian teachers formed more of a community, and we sometimes spent the night in sleeping bags at one another's apartments. Many of us were homesick, and our crowd included guys from Kunsan Airforce base. The military guys signed us on base for amazing breakfasts like we had back home.

A few weeks after my twenty-fifth birthday in early January, my roommate, Jackson, invited Rachel and me to a dinner with a competing Hagwan owner. I preferred to pick up extra tutoring classes with individual families, but Jackson was interested in working for this Hagwan owner part-time. Jackson said that the owner, Mister Kim, had insisted that Rachel and I join them. I didn't question it because I assumed Mister Kim would simply try to talk Rachel and me into working for him.

He took us to a nice restaurant within walking distance from our place and bought a bottle of whiskey for the table. Several female Korean English teachers were with him. I watched Jackson and Mister Kim do most of the drinking, as it is unusual in Korea for women to drink heavily. Perhaps the fact that I even had two drinks made Mister Kim see me differently, but two drinks only made me feel tired.

Jackson suggested that we play "spin the bottle" which I thought was ridiculous. Nonetheless, I watched for a bit as Jackson kissed some of the Korean teachers and they giggled. When I spun the bottle, it landed on Mister Kim. I kissed him to play along, but I didn't want to be with him, so I said my goodbyes. Jackson shouted something about Mister Kim sleeping on our couch, and I nodded, assuming they would all stay out late together.

I walked home to the apartment that I shared with Jackson and Rachel, reflecting on how at twenty-five years old, I felt wise, satisfied, and ridiculously homesick. I got ready for bed, read a chapter from *War and Peace,* listened to meditation music, and fell asleep. In Korea, we slept on thin futon-like beds on the floor. Most of the English teachers piled two of these on top of each other for extra padding.

However, when you put two mattresses together, you don't get as much ambient warmth from the heated floors.

When I woke up, I felt cold, and the florescent light from the bathroom filled my room. Mister Kim walked in and got on top of me before I could ask what was going on. I did not have a lock on my door, but my door was shut when I went to bed. I didn't know this at the time, but Jackson and Rachel decided to stay late that night, going all the way to the American military base to keep drinking. They gave one set of keys to Mister Kim so that he could crash on our couch. I screamed, but they weren't around to hear my scream. I pushed at him, but he slammed his elbow into my neck with surprising force, and I feared my windpipe might collapse.

I wanted to fight more, but I was afraid of injuring my back. Mister Kim was stocky, muscular, and the hit to my neck surprised me; I struggled to catch my breath. As a child, the shock I experienced from being hit taught me to be quiet and still until the moment ended, so that's what I did. I got very still and quiet.

Mister Kim pulled down my underwear and shoved his penis inside me. I lay perfectly still, disconnecting from the moment. My only thought was about other times I had enjoyed sex. I felt relieved that I wasn't a virgin and could remember happier times. This was my way of coping with the horror of the moment. He kept his hand over my mouth even though I had stopped screaming. I only looked at him once, hating him for taking away some of my power, and I wished I could run to Chip for help.

When it was over, Mister Kim got up to use the restroom, and he came back into my room as if he planned to sleep next to me. I asked him to sleep on our couch. I thought about getting a knife from the kitchen and stabbing him, but I feared the Korean police might not treat me fairly. Because of Kwang Min's horribly unfair divorce, I knew the South Korean system did not treat Korean women well, so I couldn't imagine what would happen to me as a foreigner. I wasn't sure if I should go to the American Embassy. Because I didn't know what to do, I simply waited for daylight.

That morning, Mister Kim came back into my room. I put on my glasses and hugged my legs to my chest, not bothering to answer any of his questions. He asked if last night was good for me, and if I wanted to see him again. I looked at him and hissed, "Fuck you! It was horrible, and I never want to see you again. Don't even think of setting foot in my apartment!"

I braced myself, wondering if he might hit me or kick me. Jackson and Rachel were chatting in the kitchen. The thought of kicking me seemed to cross his mind as he stepped toward me, but he stopped and studied me for a long moment and then said, "You aren't as pretty with your glasses on."

On his way out, he said his goodbyes to Jackson and Rachel, as if nothing out of the ordinary had occurred.

When I told my roommates what happened, they were quietly stunned. Because they couldn't process the event other than saying that it sucked, they mostly talked about their night. Apparently, they had continued to drink together, staying up until three a.m. When Jackson took a shower, Rachel told me that she hooked up with Jackson that night for the first time. I was annoyed by her reaction, and they reminded me of some of the immature friends who visited me in the hospital.

I needed comfort or some sort of validation to feel more grounded. I called everyone that I knew, looking for help. Jackson and Rachel drank coffee and listened to my conversations. Other teachers were either horrified or ambivalent. Some women were afraid for themselves or told me about moments of assault or rape they had already experienced in South Korea and how the police had laughed at them and called them "whores who deserved what they got."

After a couple of hours, Jackson decided that he wouldn't work for Mister Kim, as if he had thought about this all morning and decided to make the financial sacrifice because of my experience. Rachel didn't hug me or offer any support, and I felt like she didn't care. Rachel often seemed sad, walking around with slumped shoulders and a downcast head.

I wished my roommate might've been more of a friend, but after the way she handled my rape, I realized we would never be allies. Perhaps my roommates were doing the best they could as products of dysfunctional homes. Jackson and Rachel weren't interested in spirituality, religion, or much of anything other than good times. If I remember correctly, he was in a frat, and I imagined the atmosphere couldn't have been much different than the movie *Animal House*. I pictured Jackson as the type of guy who would overlook toxic male behavior; he wouldn't be a predator himself, but he wouldn't confront anyone. In many ways, I felt stronger than the two of them.

Later that afternoon, I called my beautiful friend, Kwang Min. She was the only person who showed true compassion for me, and she told me about how she was pulled from the sidewalk into a shop and raped when she was only fourteen. I learned Korean girls and women walk in pairs or in groups to stay safe. They often link arms walking down the street to avoid getting raped. I can only speculate why the girls didn't link arms with Kwang Min the day she was raped. Whatever the reason, Kwang Min walked home alone that afternoon, and a horrid shop owner raped her hurriedly and flung her back on the street.

Kwang Min recalled the event without emotion, simply saying rape was all too common and almost expected. She told me that she would make an appointment at a gynecologist and go with me. I asked about going to the police, but she said, "You're American, and you were seen drinking in public. You even kissed him. The police would laugh at you."

I knew she was right after hearing the stories of other English teachers, but I wanted to make the report anyway with the hope that attitudes might change someday. She persuaded me not to bother and took me to a gynecologist and translated for me, even staying in the room and holding my hand to make sure that the doctor treated me with respect.

As the weeks continued, my optimism and power dissipated. I was rattled, paranoid, and afraid. My hair started falling out in clumps from the stress. The trauma of the car wreck and near-death experience was much easier to process because I had a connection to angels and God, but now I wondered where my angels were. I felt frantic, disconnected, and abandoned by the angels and left to suffer in a dark world. I couldn't understand why rape could be part of the story I was brought back to experience.

I stayed up late many nights, desperately trying to make sense of the situation. I played out all the scenarios of how rape would change my life. I knew there would be many people who would blame me—the victim, even going so far as to say I brought this on myself by traveling to a foreign country or by going out drinking. I knew these people were wrong, but their judgments would hurt me. I was not responsible for the criminal behavior of others.

I immediately hated the idea of manifestation because I knew I didn't manifest rape as part of my story. In the few years since my near-death experience, I read spiritual books about how our attitude and vibration creates our reality. However, these types of books ceased to resonate with me after being raped, and if rape was part of my soul contract, then I wasn't prepared to handle it. I needed support to get through the horrifying aftereffects of rape, and these theories were deeply demoralizing to me as a victim.

Guilt wouldn't help me heal, and the only thing that seemed accurate is that rape happens to young women all over the world and the statistics are horrifying. My vibration didn't manifest a stalker or this rape; rather, collective unconscious had created rape culture—a culture that gives men power over women and doesn't often hold them responsible for violence against women should be considered the culprit. From that point forward, my power would lie in my ability to survive PTSD, to learn ways to heal, and to fight to create a safer world. If I could be blamed for anything, it was simply being a young, impulsive woman without a clear idea of my future besides enjoying the moment and teaching.

I didn't sleep more than three hours at a time for the rest of my stay in South Korea. Meditations were no longer a peaceful practice but more of an escape. When I was awake, I felt agitated and paranoid, sometimes thinking about horrible things happening across the border in North Korea.

I cried most evenings after leaving my students, not wanting to disappoint them by leaving without notice, but I feared the Hawgan wouldn't pay me if I broke the contract. When I was ready to leave the country, I would simply take my last paycheck and buy a ticket home.

* * *

While busy teaching, I forgot about my pain and poured myself into being the best possible teacher. The preschoolers' English improved exceedingly fast. When I first met them, they didn't know a word of English, but after close to seven months with me, they ran and hugged my legs each afternoon saying, "We love you, Tricia Teacher."

However, after rape, depression and anxiety kicked in as badly as before my near-death experience, and to make matters worse I contracted a case of Japanese encephalitis. I stayed in bed believing that my brain must've swollen because my eyes were solid red, and my head pounded with fierce pain. While looking for an emergency clinic, I accidentally walked into a psychiatrist's office and spilled out all my troubles to Doctor Park. He listened and commented thoughtfully and wrote a prescription for Zoloft. Doctor Park directed me to a hospital down the street to treat my flu and hired me to tutor his twin daughters. He hoped to send them to college in Washington or California, and his desire for his daughters' success touched me.

I made these two girls my special project and stopped travelling on the weekends to spend long afternoons with these spunky twins. They giggled at my warnings about men and took me roller skating at the most crowded roller-skating rinks I've ever seen. Korean children took pictures and stared at me: an adult—a tall, blonde foreigner—pulled along by the twins at ridiculously fast speeds until I felt dizzy, begging them to stop.

In my final weeks in Korea, I spent my free time with Kwang Min in the hopes of helping her find an American husband. Selfishly, I wanted our friendship to continue in the U.S. That spring the cherry blossoms arrived early, and

Zoloft made all the colors so much brighter. I noticed the dramatic change in my mood over coffee with Kwang Min. She had on a bright green sweater, and I felt certain that she was one of the most beautiful women on the planet.

When the temperatures got warmer, I booked a ticket to Seattle via Honolulu leaving on May 5. I wanted to have a vacation on my way home, hoping to ease some of my stress. I hated leaving the country without saying goodbye to my students. I would especially miss the crazy group of junior high class clowns. That class was made up mostly of boys, and these boys gave me hope for men. One boy appeared to have a crush on me and looked at me with the most innocent big brown eyes. That last week of teaching, I remember watching as he pulled money from a Mickey Mouse billfold for a snack. I hoped he would always be the kind, innocent human being I knew him to be and that he would never hit a girlfriend or wife, say awful things to a woman, or rape a woman. I couldn't believe he possibly could, but I prayed for him, for each of them, and hoped they would remember me fondly.

I felt a pure form of unconditional love for my students. I loved their many different personalities, their dreams, their silliness, their shyness, and their strength; my heart seemed stretched to its capacity with love for them. On the last afternoon with my dear little preschoolers, I couldn't hold back my tears as I hugged them goodbye. I'm sure one sweet child with a bright, fluffy hair clip intuited that she wouldn't see me again. She ran back into the classroom, hugged me hard, and looked at me for a long while with her hands on my cheeks. Her tender gaze and innocence felt healing. I thought about how the light had told me to love like a little child. If my roommates and others had loved me like a little child, I would have recovered from rape much quicker.

I only told my roommates, a few friends from the air force base, a couple of Canadian teachers, and Kwan Min the exact date of my departure, but they threw a huge party for me anyway, complete with tequila from the military base. One wild teacher pulled a few Polish sailors off the street and into the debauchery of my farewell party. The night of revelry was the closest thing to love that I could experience with this group. Even Rachel told me I looked very peaceful and hugged me goodbye.

Although it was healing to say goodbye to everyone, I felt angry at Mister Kim for traumatizing me and robbing me of the opportunity to say goodbye to the students who I loved. I didn't get to celebrate with them and enjoy a party with balloons, small gifts of thanks, cards, songs, and silly games. I didn't get to tell the sweet little preschoolers and kind adults how much I would miss them. My students' faces are burned into my memory, but I've forgotten Mister Kim's face, though not the vicious act. When we heal, love is what we keep with us, not the moments of horror.

However, on that late-night flight leaving Seoul, I remember thinking that it would probably take dying again to erase the memory of rape. I couldn't imagine how to integrate the event into my life, and my shock and anger seemed to stretch like the red line on the monitor that I watched, not sleeping, as the plane inched toward Honolulu International Airport. I was ready to forget South Korea and make new memories.

CHAPTER FOURTEEN

FALLING APART

"I just want to sleep.
A coma would be nice. Or amnesia.
Anything, just to get rid of this, these thoughts,
whispers in my mind. Did he rape my head, too?"
—Laurie Halse Anderson, Speak

Though it was evident that I was falling apart back in the U.S., I had no choice but to find work. I stayed at my friend, Clyde's house in Austin for a while, and we spent a lot of time outdoors in nature walking in state parks and through the botanical gardens. Clyde tried to bring peace to my agitated state, and one afternoon in his car when I kept vacillating between tears and deep anger as I thought about the rape and the unsupportive reactions of my roommates, he pulled over to pray and connect with his guidance. I felt him connect with divine love, and I understood that he felt my pain and wanted to relieve me of some of the intensity. I could sense his intent and it deeply touched me. I felt blessed to have those healing days with my friend, Clyde. He did Reiki work on me several times, and those sessions helped me return to enough ease within myself to fill out job applications.

As with every life experience, I simply learned who I didn't want to be and who I wanted to be. I determined that I would never recoil from another's pain as my roommates had, or worse, blame the victim. Instead, I would be present, reach out for guidance from the heavens, and give love and attention to the one in pain. I imagined that I would have plenty of students who would need my love.

A few weeks after visiting with Clyde, I found a low-paying but interesting teaching gig as an SAT preparatory skills/ study skills instructor based out of Boston. My new job would keep me on the road moving from city to city from Maine to Georgia, and I looked forward to working with students because teaching always seemed to bring light back into my life.

The owners of the business were older, and I preferred Gil to Ben. Ben was tall and snobby, and he didn't seem interested in talking to us about where we were from what we might experience on the road. However, they both rubbed me the wrong way when they talked about a tutor who they had defended. Apparently, a sixteen-year-old student informed her parents that her SAT tutor spent extra time with her in her bedroom at boarding school and made inappropriate advances. Gil and Ben said that they talked with the young man and believed he had not done anything wrong. They used the example to show those of us in training that it was probably not a bright idea to tutor students individually in their bedrooms. I thought, "Well, no shit. Who would think that is appropriate?"

From what I knew about men thus far in life, they were quite capable of making unwanted advances behind closed doors. I usually dressed like a hippie chick in baggy clothes, feeling like an average, girl next door type, not a siren or a flirt, but I had faced more harassment than I thought any woman should have to face. I believed the girl, and I hated my bosses for blindly defending the tutor. Gil and Ben obviously cared more about their business than they did about the students.

Since I had to survive, I didn't tell them what I thought of their decision. Gil seemed to like me, and he would be my main telephone contact on the road, letting me know which boarding school or which college I would need to move to every few weeks. At least, I would be someone safe for the students. At twenty-five, I could offer my students support and encouragement, hopefully gaining some insight from the wisdom of the other side.

Connecticut College in Mystic, Connecticut, was one of my first assignments, and I fell in love with the town and the lush, green expanses where students could throw blankets down to study or cuddle with one another. For the study skills course, my students were a mix of athletes and disengaged students.

A few young women immediately liked me, perhaps because of my youth and friendliness. One student attached herself to me and I welcomed the company, blessed to have a student and friend there for a couple of weeks. Jennifer and I ate tofu ice cream in her school cafeteria and talked about how she ended up at Connecticut College. With that first connection, I realized why God had guided me to this profession. In connecting with students, a part of my innocence and belief in the world returned. I could offer the kind of support that I wished I had received on my journey.

Over ice cream, my student told me about how she lived with her dad because her mom had issues with drugs and alcohol. Jennifer's father worked long hours, and she mainly entertained herself with television, movies, and video games. She got into college because of her math scores but she hated reading. I didn't know if the speed-reading and study skills course Gil and Rob had developed would help her that much, but I knew that if I told her how much she could learn and heal from reading more, she might want to read more.

I told her to research the causes of addiction and what it is like to be the child of an addict. These words came from a place I didn't consciously choose to say, and I wondered if the angels had worked through me. She perked up and said her dad took her to Alateen a few times. I listened and asked her about her dreams of being an engineer. By the time we stopped talking, I could clearly picture a good life for this intelligent young woman. When I first saw her, Jennifer had a sadness clinging to her. But talking with her that day, I noticed that her energy shifted, and I believed that I had been a small positive role in her life.

While teaching the study skills/speed reading class, I assured my students that the more they read, the faster they would read. They tried my suggestions and believed in themselves more at the end of the course. Dispelling student fears about college and giving them more confidence in their abilities may be the most important thing I accomplished in those weeks.

Each town offered interesting places to stay, and in Mystic, Connecticut I stayed in a lovely room for rent. The retired couple usually offered the room to visiting Unity ministers. They invited me to their church, and the songs and loving environment uplifted my spirit. This couple was so moved by my near-death experience story that they offered pay for me to become a Unity minister. I thanked them but reminded them that God said I had to teach. I was sad to leave their charming home and the safety of their guest bedroom.

While on the road, each group of students taught me something and healed something in me as I gave back to them. At Tilton boarding school in New Hampshire, some of the students offered me money to buy beer for them. They were disappointed when I wouldn't accept the money and assured me that they would pay someone in town to buy the beer. I could've used an extra hundred dollars, but I wanted to interact with students in uplifting ways.

I walked with one of them into town and told him that teaching was a holy profession to me. Though I might make mistakes in the rest of my life, I wanted to be there for my students' souls' journeys in any small way. I asked him what it was like living at boarding school. He told me a little about his life and how much time he spent with teachers there, even in the evenings.

When we reached the store, he easily convinced an older man standing outside of the store to buy the beer, and as he walked off, he suggested that I should meet them at their party. I felt lonely and isolated from my friends in Austin and San Antonio but drinking with my underage students sounded like a horrible idea. I thought about how that tutor might have felt that the sixteen-year old girl was mature for her age and felt lonely. I didn't have as much judgment for him as I did the first time I heard the story, but I felt good about myself for keeping appropriate boundaries and working for the betterment of my students' souls. Every time I heard about a teacher crossing boundaries with students, I felt sad that they didn't see their potential to influence a student's life in a positive way.

Later, at another small, beautiful boarding school, dressed up in the red, gold, and yellow leaves of fall, I sipped my coffee one morning and couldn't help feeling sorry for myself, especially about the pitifully small paycheck I received every two weeks.

As I wallowed in self-pity, one of my beautiful, dark-haired students walked by, dragging her leg along the sidewalk. Sara had a massive stroke at sixteen that left her with very little use of the left side of her face and body. As I watched her struggle to walk across the lawn, I noticed she had a smile on her face and hope radiating through her being. You can't fake that kind of optimism. Seeing her joy jolted me out of my self-pity and I walked slowly to class, consciously working on improving my mindset by making a mental gratitude list.

Because of Sara's optimism, I dedicated myself to doing everything I could to contribute to her success. While helping Sara and other students, my dark thoughts fell effortlessly away from me. Concerning myself with the needs of others freed me from the weight of my own story.

Love and unconditional appreciation of my students shaped their experiences in my classroom and accomplished more than other lessons, and I knew that the beautiful flower of Sara's bright happy face would show up on the saddest days of my future. She blessed me with her optimism. The light of God must have known that my students would heal me as much as I healed them. If I continued to show up for work, divine miracles would happen in my life and in the lives of others.

* * *

During my stint with Gil and Ben's company, I travelled to so many different boarding schools and colleges that I eventually felt ungrounded. I loved being in the classroom with students, but I wondered if I should settle in one area and find supportive friends.

At Washington and Lee University, I attended a rape awareness event, and four different women talked about their experience as rape survivors. After the talk, I met with one woman who was raped in Africa while she worked for the Peace Corps. Her energetic body seemed to have a big, traumatic hole shot through it, and I wondered if my own energetic being looked the same way. She seemed to recognize my pain, and she hugged me for a long while, emphatically suggesting that I quit my traveling job and live somewhere where I could participate in a support group. I appreciated her concern, but I wanted to finish my teaching assignment.

While teaching in Virginia, I had time to hike and meditate in the forests. *Remind them to go to nature* was one of the messages that I heard during my near-death experience, so I spent time in nature, hoping to heal some of my own wounds. On mountaintops, I lay prostrate begging that my power and energy return, but I usually felt like a sacrificial lamb. The trees gave me some energy and strength as I stood against various ones, asking for strength.

One afternoon, I hiked near the Shenandoah Valley and meditated on a rock for a long while. At some point during the meditation, I felt the presence of several Native American spirits. One man stepped forward and communicated telepathically, "*Please don't forget about us. Remember us.*"

I felt honored that his spirit wanted me to help preserve the memory of his people. However, I didn't understand why this wise-looking man picked me. Maybe he picked me simply because I could see him. I decided to teach Native American literature in every English class. I would use quotes from *Black Elk Speaks* and talk about the wisdom from Native American cultures whenever possible. I later learned that history of Native Americans dated back over eleven thousand years in that area. The land held their memories, and as I hiked through those beautiful woods, I felt the presence of a civilization before ours, a civilization in touch with the workings of nature.

* * *

At some point during my travels, I began to stay up most of the night. My creativity was heightened, and I wrote lots of journal entries, but memories of the rape disturbed me. I was asleep when my rapist entered my room, so sleep became the enemy. Since I had to stay in cheap motels or little dinky rental rooms, I kept a knife on every nightstand or under my pillow, often practicing how quickly I could wake and ready myself for a fight.

I didn't have just any knife on my nightstand; I had a fighting knife with a long ergonomic handle and deep finger grooves. I bought it at an army surplus store when I knew I'd be traveling for a living. Most nights, I dragged furniture or my suitcase in front of the door. If nothing else, I put a couple of glass bottles in front of the door so that I would hear an intruder.

After the first snow, I stayed indoors more often, subsisting on packets of tea and diet pills because I didn't want to spend much of my salary on food. One night as I played with my knife, practicing how to grab it quickly, I thought about how so much had happened in my life and how I honestly didn't have time to process it all. I thought about the friend, Blake, I had mistakenly trusted while visiting Iowa City. Before I returned home to Austin from hiking in Maine with Chip, I took a bus to Iowa City to check out the city. Chip flew back home, but I wanted to extend my summer vacation. Also, I knew that the University of Iowa's MFA program was one of the best in the country, and I wanted to see if I could handle living in the Midwest.

Blake, a guy from a writing group in Austin, assured me that he was over his crush on me and that I could sleep on his couch. I thought of Blake as a friend, mainly because he had been kind enough to visit me in the hospital. When I arrived in his town, he took me directly back to his apartment and offered me a massage. My back hurt, so I said yes. Quickly, the massage lingered in uncomfortable, sexual ways, so I jumped up and insisted he show me the town, hoping to break the awkwardness of the moment.

Once we started walking around town looking at various statues, I reiterated that nothing would happen sexually between us, reminding him that I had an awesome boyfriend. He got angry and talked incessantly about how he wanted to go down on me and give me slow, seductive oral sex. He furiously asked if I visited just to taunt him, but I argued that he promised I could crash on the couch. He knew how interested I was in attending that graduate school.

Looking back now, I should've run out of his apartment with or without my things, even if I had to stay awake all night in the bus station. At the time, I felt caught in a panicked loop of trying to reason with him. I begged Blake to stop mentioning anything sexual. I even wrote out a list of words that were unacceptable and asked him if it were possible to forget his attraction and be kind enough to let me stay one night.

He pouted and called a couple of his friends, and we all met at a bar. I ignored Blake most of the night out and talked with his guy friends; I even asked one of his friends who lived with his girlfriend if I could stay on his couch. The guy called his girlfriend, but she wasn't down for that situation.

When I thought about that night, I wanted to go back in time and shake myself into becoming more threatening or self-protective. Why did I think I could reeducate Blake or teach him how to behave better? I didn't teach him anything, and the night only got stranger. When we were at the bar, Blake called me over to where he was standing at the end of the bar near the woman's restroom and said, "Whenever I stand here in the 'alpha male spot' in this bar, I can have any woman I want. I can probably have you."

He was drunk, egotistical, and mentally unstable, a much sicker man than I realized. I wanted to believe that the light gave me the power to help others, even people in grip of madness. If I would've known the abusive vitriol I would experience once we got back to his apartment, I never would've entered. He screamed about what a whore I was for talking with his guy friends and flirting with them. He threw a beer bottle across his kitchen, saying, "I deserve a fuck from you for as many people as you've probably fucked anyway."

I was scared to move. If I started packing my things up, I thought he might try to stop me violently. When he went to the restroom, I grabbed a butcher knife from the kitchen and put it under my pillow on his couch. My rage surprised me. I felt fully prepared to kill him if he tried to rape me, but I was also too scared to walk out and face him without the element of surprise.

I stayed up most of the night with my hand on the knife. Blake got up at one point, plugged in his electric guitar, turned on all the lights and played the Muddy Water's song "Got My Mojo Working." The florescent lights from his kitchen were intensely bright, but I actually liked the song and tapped my foot to it with my hand on the knife thinking, “Yep, this man is crazy as fuck. He is crazy as fuck.”

As he sang the lyrics, I couldn’t help thinking he did have little talent. I tried to find a place of compassion, wondering if this is the best he knew how to be in his life. My near-death experience made me want to envision the best for others, and even in this ridiculous moment I hoped he eventually found peace and sanity.

After Blake slammed the bedroom door, I assumed he made his point. I didn’t want to fall asleep, but I dozed off somewhere around four a.m. and awoke at seven a.m. to see his face only a few inches from mine. Who knows how long he had been staring at me as I slept? I let out a startled scream, forgetting about the knife for a moment, and then I slowly moved my hand under the pillow and gripped the handle, thinking, *Touch me, asshole, and I am plunging this knife into your neck.*

Luckily, he went for a jog, and I immediately called a taxi to meet me across the street. After I finished a brief run-down of my time in her city, the taxi driver lit a cigarette, opened her window, and said, “Girl, you’re the crazy one for thinking that man might behave. Never trust a man to behave when no one is watching.”

Though I realized what a mistake it was to have stayed at Blake’s apartment, I hated to think that I couldn’t trust any man enough to be my friend.

During sleepless nights I thought long and hard about that night and about the things I might have done differently. Most of all, I could have listened to my intuition that told me that Blake seemed too eager for me to visit. Since applying for the graduate program in his town was out of the question, I didn't know where I wanted to attend graduate school or what I wanted to do after this teaching assignment. I felt fragile and lost, much like all the maple leaves falling from trees and blowing about randomly.

Blake wasn't the only situation that played in my mind those isolated nights on the road. I thought about the weird men in Austin who masturbated on the lawn. While completing my student teaching, I rented one of five rooms in a gorgeous house near a row of sorority homes. A couple of different middle-aged men prowled these areas of Austin, hoping to get a glimpse of young women changing. The women in these houses grew accustomed to calling the cops when we spotted a "water sprinkler" as we jokingly called the masturbators.

However, it ceased to be funny the night our house was broken into and we each locked our doors from the inside, listening in silent fear as the intruder walked through the house, trying each of our doors. I kept a knife in my room then too, and I remember sitting against the wall, barely breathing and poised to pounce if my door was busted down.

I thought about the creepy guy, Dave, from the poetry reading and the package he sent to South Korea. Even without taking the rape into account, these moments seemed overwhelming. If I went back farther in time and thought about other situations, I felt dizzy. I couldn't reach far enough back into my unconscious to remember why I hated my Uncle Darin so much at the tender age of four, but I know that I spent my childhood and teenage years wanting to protect my little cousins from him.

I also felt angry with my bosses. They had power over predators, and they could have protected other students by firing the tutor who wronged the student. Toward the end of my contract, I called Gil and told him that I could no longer continue working for him because of the aftereffects of rape. I didn't tell him exactly when I had been raped, and I hoped that he thought it was while I worked for his company. I wanted him to think about how his company and the bottom line shouldn't mean more than the student's complaint. I also wanted him to think about paying their tutors a salary high enough to ensure safer living arrangements.

Gil and I determined that Atlanta would be my last assignment, mainly because I had a friend who lived there. My good friend, Nina, recently moved to Atlanta with her lover, Tabitha, and I felt thrilled to finally connect with a friend. However, when I arrived at her door, Nina looked displeased and told me I looked too skinny. Most models taller than me weigh less than the 120 pounds I weighed at the time; I didn't feel my weight was an issue. I felt great and loved how my clothes hung loosely from my body. Skinny equaled cool and tough in my mind.

After a few days of hanging out in Buckhead, I broke down and told Nina about the rape. She shook her head and said, "That is so sad. Tricia, I know that you are really suffering, but you have to take this seriously and get help."

She suggested that I go to The Rape Crisis Center, and I hated her for insisting that I call my mother and return to Texas. We watched a stack of movies until Mom swooped into Atlanta, a day after Nina called my mother to explain my mental and physical state. On the drive back to San Antonio, Mom and I made an odd pilgrimage to Monticello, Gettysburg, and other historical tourist destinations. I walked through Confederate graves sites, briefly browsing through the brochures for highlights. Nothing mattered. I wanted to feel better.

As we neared San Antonio with Mom driving most of the way in my cheap little blue Mazda that transported me all over the East Coast, she told me that she had contacted The Rape Crisis Center. I bristled but promised to give the place a try. I wanted to move on from the experience, maybe even forget about it, not process rape in little groups of sad women. Even on the drive, Mom annoyed me with her discussions about rape. She decided that she hated God for letting this happen to me and had lost faith in God. My rape became her spiritual crisis, and I couldn't deal with her breakdown. I had my own to process.

The Rape Crisis Center was worse than I imagined. I picked up on the emotions of others, and the weight of sorrow in that room felt like it could drown me. I could barely breathe. I didn't want to add my story to the broken pile of sad stories, but the other women looked at me expectantly. Their curious eyes wanted to know the specifics of my story, but I refused to speak. I knew that would be the only meeting I ever attended. I would tell Mom that I was going to The Rape Crisis Center, but I would walk around downtown, go to one of the art museums, or get a drink and talk with locals instead.

When I walked out of group therapy that day, I saw a young Hispanic girl who couldn't have been more than nine or ten years old with long brown braids on each side of her puffy, tear-stained cheeks. The horror of what had happened to her immediately entered my body. I felt the shock, shame, and confusion that she felt, and I wanted to kill her rapist. I've never felt more rage in my life, and I stormed out of The Rape Crisis Center. I turned the radio up loud and drove outside of town to the only deserted place I could find—a quarry.

No one was working at the time, so I pulled my car alongside a caterpillar and walked to the edge. I picked up rocks and threw them into the quarry and screamed and cried until my voice became hoarse and raspy, and I could barely talk. I told myself this was the therapy I needed. I raged and screamed at God until the sun set. Exhausted, I eventually sat in my car in the darkness. I felt angels all around me offering comfort, but I didn't want to listen to them. I felt betrayed and left alone in a cruel world, a world that had been cruel to women for so long, a world where Native Americans were slaughtered unfairly and tried to contact our generation through a messed-up person like me.

How was I going to help them? How was I going to help other women? My gender seemed an unfair cross to bear, and I missed what it felt like to shed my gender and be a spirit. In a small place in my heart, I hoped that whatever I survived I could eventually use to help transform the world. Maybe I could teach many young people how to be more sensitive and empathetic with one another. Maybe I could even prevent rape with my story. Despite my anger, I continued to believe that the other side had a reason for asking me to return and work as a teacher.

CHAPTER FIFTEEN

NEW ORLEANS

"The blues was bleeding the same blood as me."
—B.B. King

After a few weeks back in San Antonio, Mom suggested that I attend graduate classes at UTSA, and I figured academia would add more balance to my life. However, UTSA's program felt like a mix of my high school English classes and undergraduate classes. The creative writing workshops were so awful that they seemed like something out of a sitcom. I missed Austin and the poetry slams, conversations, and seemingly instantaneous friendships.

I looked for stimulation in other places, and I quickly found someone to take my mind off my problems. My flashy distraction had a name—Scott Belfour, a broad-shouldered Texan with a boisterous sense of humor and mischievous eyes. I might as well have thrown a dart at a map when it came time to pick a husband. I couldn't have picked a worse mate. I think I picked him because he seemed protective of me when we first met, but I probably mistook control for security.

We were only married a year, and when I think about that horrible year I remind myself that no matter how bad things got for me, my life always made sense in the classroom, even if only for a month-long substitute position in a tough school district just outside of the New Orleans city limit. Scott also helped me find a low-residency graduate program out of Vermont that fit my creative needs more than UTSA, and for that I felt gratitude.

Scott and I ended up in New Orleans via Boston—all for his career. After Scott confessed to wanting an open marriage, I hid out writing poetry in coffee houses in the Quarter. Scott avoided me too, spending his lavish expense account faster than the money hit his bank account. I knew I had to divorce him, but graduate school was taking up a great deal of my time, and I needed to plan for my future.

Scott moved in with a friend and gave me a month in our house to figure out what to do. I lived at a slower pace than Scott, matching myself to a different rhythm and watching the barn owls, egrets, and alligators in ponds on the golf course where we lived. Some days, I walked slowly from Dauphine to Decatur, occasionally catching the lost, mournful notes of a valve trombone.

I considered staying in the New Orleans area, and took a long-term substitute teaching position, hoping they might offer me a full-time position the next year. I was assigned a junior class that had run off *twelve* other substitute teachers. On the day that I applied for the position, the principal looked me over, and I could see that she didn't believe I would have any luck with the class. However, I knew that any opportunity in the classroom meant that the light could pour into my life and theirs, even during a short-term assignment.

I imagined that the students would not listen to me if I tried to talk with them, so I walked in the classroom, put my feet up on the desk, and started reading a book, not even bothering to glance at them. I pretended to read for thirty minutes while they talked loudly, visiting with one another and milling around the trailer. Eventually, one tall, young man with shoulder-length dreadlocks walked up to my desk and said, "You aren't even going to bother to teach us, are you?"

I replied, "The principal let me know that you've run off *twelve* other substitutes, so teaching your class is obviously a joke. I need the money to get away from my abusive husband who bashed my head against a wall when I filed for divorce. He probably sleeps with a different woman every night. I thought I'd let you do whatever you want as long as you don't burn the place down."

My student laughed at my honesty and introduced himself as Wayne. He asked if I had a degree, and I told him I was in graduate school and studying poetry. Wayne wrote his own songs and raps, occasionally performing his music in clubs. After chatting with me for a while, Wayne decided that he wanted to hear what I would teach their class *if* I had their attention.

I recognized the same maturity in him that I possessed at his age. You don't get that kind of maturity from having an easy life. I could tell he carried the world on his shoulders from the little bits of conversation we shared. From that very first day of class, I was grateful to Wayne for wanting to hear what I had to say about poetry. Wayne had enough credibility and charisma to quiet the room, and I spent the next weeks giving them my best lessons. They wrote creatively for me, and I worked individually with each student to improve their writing.

One somber young man wrote a narrative about his mother. His mother had shot her ex-boyfriend in the leg and he returned to her, never telling the cops. She shot him again in the same leg, and a few months later the boyfriend returned to her. I probably asked forty different questions about this young man's life, and he answered them quietly with his eyes focused on the ground.

I made him promise to keep writing about his life and to write his way out of that life. I did my best to give him some light to guide him to a new place in life. For a few magical moments, I watched his face transform as he looked at me, believing that I saw something special in him. I couldn't believe that it took so little effort on my part to open his heart a bit. All I had to do was see any one of my students, really see him or her, and then offer some hope—not a ton of hope, either—just a thread.

This student with the trigger-happy mother knew that I believed in him, and I did. I honestly did, despite his situation. I prayed for him more than I prayed for myself. I reminded this shy, talented kid that he could find a way out of that madness and that education might very well be his way out. He was one of the better writers because he often locked himself in his room and read books.

My students were a largely guarded, distrustful crowd of students, and I didn't blame them after hearing about some of their home lives. Somehow, my silliness and honesty opened them up to me. I connected with their hope for a better life, and we worked hard together. I promised them that in a month I could teach them more than many English teachers would teach them all year if they would only concentrate, not be afraid to make mistakes, and learn new things. I convinced them that I wanted nothing more than their success, and their respect felt sacred and rare.

Each morning, I stood outside the trailer before entering, asking for the ancestors of all these young people to assist me. My goodness, New Orleans is full of ghosts and ancestors. Sometimes that trailer felt crowded to the brim, but the class wrote and revised four essays in my time with them. They tore through worksheets and creative prompts, and they proved their writing abilities and earned my respect.

I made it to the end of their school year, and Wayne secretly asked the principal to stop by on my last day. She showed up and the class—mainly Wayne and a small group of students—performed a song for me about how they had run off all twelve of the subs, but not me. They listed the attributes of the other subs in somewhat negative terminology, but the gist of the song was "not her, not her, not her, we liked her." One girl's beautiful voice rang out wishing me a happy life and classrooms full of students. I wished that I had a year with them instead of only a month.

Despite the students' performance, the principal didn't have a job for me, and when I received my final paycheck, I realized that it wasn't enough to get an apartment or even move my furniture back to Texas. I stopped on the side of the road to cry and beg the heavens for a quick way out of my marriage. Since Scott shut off all my access to the bank accounts, I didn't know if he would even give me money for a U-Haul.

Out of nowhere, I felt my grandfather's presence, and I followed his guidance, driving down a backroad I'd never seen before. A few miles outside of town, I spotted a jewelry shop. I'd been considering pawning my wedding ring, so I asked the owner if he would consider purchasing a year-old wedding ring. He inspected my ring carefully and said, "I'll polish it up and sell it online."

He quickly handed me one thousand dollars, and I thanked him excitedly. The money would be enough to get me back to Texas. Before my grandfather died of leukemia, he gave me a hundred dollars, ten dollars for each of my ten years hoping that I would remember him. He didn't know that I had prayed to God and as a test, asked for a hundred dollars, because I told no one. I felt connected to him again.

After-death communication with my grandfather felt ordinary for me; after all, I had recently seen him in the afterlife. My grandfather asked me to call Dad, and I told Dad about Scott's two different moments of physical violence. Dad confidently assured me that Scott would never touch me again. He told me to drive home and put the phone on speaker if Scott was there. Scott usually stayed at his friend's house, but he happened to be at our house that day. I walked in with a new assertiveness, shut off the television, and told Scott my dad wanted to talk with him.

Scott feared no one, and I could tell he thought he would have the upper hand in that conversation. In a casual, relaxed tone of voice, Dad described what he would do to Scott if he ever laid a hand on me again. Dad said he would come up behind Scott and that Scott would never see him coming. The last thing Scott would feel would be a tire tool hitting him hard on the back of the head. Dad described how he would toss his body in the trunk and use duct tape to shut off his airway. He described how he would tie a few large rocks to Scott's body and throw him in a swamp where a few of his buddies had already dumped bodies.

Dad very slowly and menacingly said, “Scott, I’m old enough and have seen enough of this life. It is very easy to kill a man. I learned that in Vietnam, and I’ll hardly bat an eyelash over killing you. I’ll do my best not to get caught, but if I do, I don’t mind serving time for Tricia. She’s my only child, and I’m probably going to get cancer soon anyway. Haven’t had the best diet, you know, and she’s my only flesh and blood left.”

Shaken, Scott said, “Okay, sir,” and hung up the phone.

He turned to me and said, “Your dad is frightening. Seriously. I don’t get intimidated by people, but he sounded glib and scary as shit.”

After Dad’s call, Scott talked to me as if I were a buddy and not the woman he promised to love until he died. He talked in a lighthearted tone about women he met recently—hairdressers who showed him they weren’t wearing underwear while cutting his hair and young women in college who danced with him at a new bar located in the French Quarter. I understood now that he had been meeting women this way while we were married, and I no longer felt shell-shocked. In some strange way, I thought that he was trying to love everyone the way I loved everyone, only he was trying to do through his wounded sexuality.

I recalled a brief telephone conversation with Scott’s brother, Grayson, who was my good friend at U.T. I called Grayson after the first date with Scott. Grayson reminded me that I shouldn’t date him, simply stating that Scott had the charisma of Jim Jones and this wasn’t a good thing. I didn’t take Grayson’s warnings seriously, but I wish I had.

The world loved to laugh with Scott, and Scott was wild about me in the beginning. He also reacted the way I thought someone should react to the fact that I had been raped. Scott wanted to fly to South Korea and kill my rapist. In truth, I didn't want to set foot in South Korea again, but in my angry phase of recovery, his reaction felt right.

When we first met, Scott made me feel safe, and I desperately wanted to feel safe. I would have never guessed that two weeks after our marriage he would repeatedly bash my head into the console of the car because I refused to give him directions to a party after he called me a bitch for accidently dinging his car door. I would have never guessed that two counselors would tell us that our marriage still had hope, and that Scott's neighbors, who were married fifteen years, would tell us a story about how early in their marriage they had fought viciously. The man told me a story about how he had thrown a ketchup bottle at his wife and it shattered on her. They claimed to never have experienced a moment of violence after that moment. Their story might have been fabricated to help Scott's case, but it encouraged me enough to stay with him.

I wish I had known better, known the unlikelihood that Scott would never use violence again. When he was violent again after close to year of living together, I tried to press charges, but since I didn't have any broken bones or visible bruises except for a bump on my head, the police department decided only to write down my complaint.

After hearing the decision from an officer, I felt connected to all the women who found themselves complexly tied to an abusive spouse. There was no doubt in my mind that if we had kids, Scott would have insisted on full custody, making up lies about me. He would have been a horrible role model, and our kids would have grown up angry, longing for my love and not able to see me often. I felt my imagined kids as if they were real. I suffered and cried for days, not only for myself but for every woman with a much worse story than mine. In my case, the worst-case scenario would be that I would have to regroup in San Antonio.

While figuring out how to get a divorce, I had a moment of fearing that I couldn't handle graduate school in this state of mind and called my professor in Paris, France, letting him know that I might not be able to continue with classes. Goddard College is a low-residency MFA program, and I had already completed the in-person workshops and time with my professor and fellow classmates.

My professor asked, "Are you going to let this god-awful husband take graduate school away from you too, or can you find a way to concentrate on your studies and forget about him? Focus on your work, Tricia."

I chuckled a little at his logical approach and promised that I would do my best to take myself seriously. My professor's advice struck me as helpful, and I imagined that I would give the same advice to my students in the future.

After Dad's call, Scott suggested we call off our lawyers and use a lawyer his friend knew back in San Antonio. The new lawyer would draw up a basic no-fault divorce decree, and I agreed.

I didn't want to return to Mom's place, but financially I didn't have another option. When Scott was violent the first time, I had called her frantically asking if she would help me. As she hung up the phone, her only reply was, "You made your bed, Tricia, you go lie in it."

Since Scott refused to give me enough money for a deposit for an apartment, I called Mom and asked if I could stay with her for a while. I don't know if Dad called Mom and insisted that she help me, or if she simply felt like helping me. Whatever the case, Mom and Jim let me move back into their house, and it felt heavenly to go to bed early and far away from Scott. I worked on my essays and creative work for graduate school late into the night, and thought about my teaching mission. I binged on self-help and spiritual books. I read about a new movement in psychology—positive psychology—and I wrote out better versions of my life for myself.

I knew I had a lot of healing work to do. The trauma in South Korea and the trauma of being married to Scott left pieces of me stuck in the past. I didn't know how to retrieve these wounded parts of myself, but I wanted to learn how to heal. Finally, I committed to getting help at the Rape Crisis Center and took more advanced self-defense classes including weapon training.

I felt hopeful about my future as a teacher. Even that one glimpse of students in New Orleans strengthened my resolve to be in the lives of students. Those students had much tougher life situations than I did, and I had the ability to remind them of their talent and their strength. I felt God working through me even in the middle of such a disturbing time. I couldn't wait to have a classroom of my own students.

CHAPTER SIXTEEN

HIGH SCHOOL SENIORS

"I am larger, better than I thought;
I did not know I held so much goodness."
—Walt Whitman, Leaves of Grass

Back in San Antonio once again, I needed to find a teaching job quickly. I applied for English positions in Austin and San Antonio, surprised by how long some of the lines were to visit with the principals of popular high schools. News cameras were on site to capture our job search. Though I was one of the people featured on the nightly news, shaking the hand of one of the principals of a large high school, I didn't get a job in Austin.

Several friends and acquaintances caught the segment on the news and called to see if I was moving back to Austin. I had to inform them, rather sadly, that I found a position south of San Antonio. The position offered a very low salary of twenty-four thousand dollars, but I could teach twelfth graders and a community college class through a distance-learning program. I had enough graduate hours through my low-residency graduate program to teach English 1301, and I imagined that teaching a class of high school seniors would prepare me for teaching at the college level.

My principal spoke plainly, honestly, and from the heart. It was obvious to me that she cared deeply about her students. The green pastures near the school reminded me of my near-death experience, and I felt God's presence with me as I signed the contract. *Finally,* I thought to myself, *I will have the opportunity to teach full time and draw on the light of the universe to come through my lectures and interactions.*

With such a low salary, I had no choice but to continue to live at Mom's house. This turned out to be a blessing because the little corgi that Scott and I had adopted stayed with my mom and stepdad while I worked all day. They were good company for my dog, and I was hardly ever there. Mom did my laundry, made dinner for me, and I worked on my graduate classes late into the night, emailing and faxing work to professors in Paris, New York, and San Francisco. After my nightmare of a marriage, I was happy to be alone and single, and even happier to have a chance to create a more grounded life.

I didn't feel nervous on the first day of classes. In fact, I felt ecstatic to have a group of seniors who would be mine for a year, all with the bonus of not having to deal with a bitter supervising teacher looking over my shoulder. I said a prayer that the angels would work through me each day, and I visualized being open to this possibility.

The students quickly cured me of any remaining naivety. During one of the first reading assignments, John raised his hand and called me over to his desk. He spoke very softly and asked me to come closer. I bent in a little closer, and then he looked at me with his big brown eyes and said, "A little closer please. I'm feeling hot for teacher."

The class erupted into laugher, and I laughed as well saying, "Okay, John is a grown man. You are all grown-ups and know how to flirt. I get it. Though what he did is not appropriate, I'm so happy that John has shown me that you are adults. Now we are going to start writing essays and working hard like adults who want to get accepted into great colleges."

The class moaned, and several people said, "Thanks a lot, John."

A week before the first big football game, I failed the entire football team's first essay, and the coaches lined up outside my door in horror when the three-week's report came out. They begged me to let the students rewrite the essays.

I replied, "Absolutely not. Their essays were ridiculously bad. Two were plagiarized with the URL still at the top of the page."

The coaches shuffled uneasily from one foot to another, scratching their heads for a retort that seemed to elude them. These two men were nicknamed "Theater Two" and "Theater Three" because of all the movies they showed in classes. I even heard that one honors European History class watched *Revenge of the Titans* a grand total of three times that year.

Feeling some compassion for the two confused men in front of me, I relented and said, "If they can miss one morning practice and rewrite the essays, editing and perfecting them, we can make this a learning experience."

The coaches nodded and walked away, visibly relieved but not happy about the missed practice.

That year, I decorated my classroom with memorabilia from Korea, and my students asked me how Korean students were different from American students. I told them that in Korea all the students bowed to me, erased my boards, and brought me water, candy, or medicine when I was sick. I told them about how their families often made me dinner and brought hot, spicy soups and rice to my classroom when I had a break.

They roared with laughter saying, "We're never going to bow to you, Miss. You're going to miss those students."

I told them I would love them just as much anyway, which brought forth a united set of moans and rolled eyes. When the football players showed up the next morning to rewrite their essays, they brought breakfast tacos, coffee, donuts, and a salad for my lunch. A few of them even wrote me notes, apologizing for their plagiarized essays. They stood in a line and bowed to me. I laughed and said, "I'm impressed! And thanks. Now, you guys have to write something that doesn't make me want to vomit up all this food."

I liked being silly with these kids, and when they turned in their make-up essays, they all had a much better product. After that morning together, I also understood more about their lives and their love of football. Some of these guys had rough home lives, and coaches did some of their best work after school when they drove certain kids home, making sure they stayed in football.

A few weeks later, on the morning of September 11, 2001, I entered my classroom early. That morning, locusts and grasshoppers jumped around madly outside the school building. Something felt amiss in the world, something indescribably elusive. During first period, despite the rules about cell phones in class, one of my students pulled out his phone. He didn't raise his hand, instead he just blurted out, "The twin towers just fell. Airplanes flew into them. I don't think it was an accident."

Instantly, I realized that America would soon be at war, and this incredibly hyperactive student in front of me started to look more like a man. I knew that this was how the Air Force, Army, Navy, and Marines would start viewing him, and this terrified me.

The entire class fell silent for a few beats until I said, "I want to know what's going on as much as you do. So, let's pretend to do research in the library, and you can watch the news on the computers."

I walked around from desk to desk, watching CNN reports and the instant replays, talking with my students about their reactions. A few parents came to the school to take their son or daughter home, especially families from military backgrounds.

As a class, we bonded in a way that I could not have imagined. Each of us would remember that class period for the rest of our lives. During the school year, I scowled at various recruiting officers standing outside of the door to my class, eagerly waiting to talk with my students. Most of my students were poor and Hispanic. Many would be first generation college students, and I wanted them to apply for scholarships and attend college.

The Marines at my door stood in the way of my hopes and dreams for my students; they offered something that could lead to potential dismemberment or even death to my kids. My kids! I did not care how patriotic my students might have felt; my goal was to keep my students alive. Knowing what I know now about their choices and how events played out, I realize that I was sensing the trauma and real danger that would later occur in some of their lives.

* * *

Early in the semester, the principal told me a story about one of my student's homes. The father, an alcoholic and diabetic who was nearly blind, stayed at two different bars late into the night. Often, the electricity company disconnected their electricity due to unpaid balances. They had no washer or dryer. The floors were made of dirt. My principal brought my student and his younger sister a new change of uniform khakis and white shirts, and she took their dirty laundry.

She initiated the uniform policy so that the extremely poor kids could blend in better and at least have clean clothes. She bought many extra uniforms and kept them in the gym, and the gym teacher did the laundry in his off period. After a few more stories like this, she enlisted me into tutoring in an afternoon program she wanted to start. The previous group of seniors had a 25 percent dropout rate, and she wanted to bring this down. She believed that the grants for better technology—iBoards and laptops—would be part of the solution. The next part would be keeping the kids at school longer and letting them get to know me and other teachers in more informal settings.

Two to three days out of the week, I stayed several hours after school, missing the afternoon traffic and sometimes simply babysitting students who played games on laptops. It was clear they didn't want to go home, and I didn't pry too much. I asked them about their dreams and gave them practical ways to work toward achieving these dreams. I helped them learn a few study techniques and tricks. We talked about test anxiety and how to become more prepared and confident going into tests.

The tutoring I had done on the East Coast at boarding schools worked well with these students. At the time, I didn't realize how successful that year truly was. The previous class had close to a 25 percent dropout rate, but my group of seniors lost only one student.

J.J. was in a gang and openly admitted to running drugs across the Texas-Mexico border. I wouldn't let him talk about it with me in the tutoring sessions. He had a silly sense of humor, and I wanted him to be a kid for a while. J.J. was sweet and quiet in my class, and ironically, it wasn't his gang activities that got him kicked out of school. He got kicked out for peeing in a trashcan in shop class. I wanted to yell at the shop teacher for not allowing him to go to the bathroom. We were so close to having a 100 percent retention rate. When the principal sent J.J. to an alternative school, he dropped out instead. He had a 72 percent in my class and might've graduated.

Though I couldn't win them all, I tried. I prayed for J.J. and the rest of my students. I prayed for the guy in special ed who told me he pleased a fifty-year-old woman in bed on occasion with oral sex, assuring me that if he could do that for her, he could certainly do that for me. I reported his statement to the administrators, but I also talked about what was appropriate and what was not appropriate to say and do in life. I told him that he deserved the love of someone his own age and that it was better to be alone sometimes and wait for the right person.

When I started the job, I had no idea that seventeen- and eighteen-year-old boys would flirt with a twenty-nine-year-old woman. Mostly, they wanted to cause a distraction, but they were also silly and completely distracted by their hormones. The media frequently covers instances where young female teachers are sexual predators; however, these young men were unbelievably, shockingly flirtatious. Teacher training, both in college and at the district level, should discuss these uncomfortable realities to better prepare teachers.

Obviously, I didn't flirt back with my students, but I laughed more often than I documented their antics. In retrospect, I should have documented everything. I'll never forget the three guys who took my keys at lunch, and then lined up against the wall, hands spread out, saying "Why don't you search us, Miss? Feel free to put your hands wherever you want to put them."

I informed these three clowns that they couldn't eat lunch in my room anymore and walked out into the cafeteria to talk with one of my senior girls who was pregnant for the second time. Though the guys dominated some of my time, the young women were the ones I longed to mentor. The young men made me laugh, and the young women made me work harder to win their admiration. Their compliments touched my heart. Even when they did not care for the literature, they told me that they trusted me and knew I wanted to help them. They told me about their dreams and their fears. Their trust was like finding a diamond ring in an abandoned field—both unexpected and miraculous.

Toward the end of the school year, I told each class about my near-death experience. My hyperactive student who had informed us all about 9/11 looked at me, mouth agape and eyes widened with shock.

"You were actually dead, Miss?" one of the quieter girls in the back asked.

"For approximately two and a half minutes," I replied. "Two of the longest and most conscious-altering moments of my life."

"Angels?" asked the inquisitive, excited voice of another student. "You saw angels? They exist?"

I told them about the healing waves of light that the angels had sent into my body. The mood of the class changed dramatically as I told my story. The class clowns stopped trying to get me off topic. The girls writing notes to their boyfriends timidly raised their hands to ask me questions about the afterlife. We spent the rest of the class period talking about their paranormal experiences.

They told me ghost stories, shared their beliefs, and though we were off-topic, we transitioned into a peaceful space for that day. The vibe of the class had changed, and they innocently and openly wondered if God had sent me back for them. I reminded them to appreciate the small moments in their life—dinner that night, petting their dog, chatting with their younger siblings, or helping their parents with household chores. A few of the students even exhibited a growing awareness and wonder about what the light's purpose might be for their lives. I wondered if simply telling this story was part of my afterlife mission. My story allowed us to bond in a new way, a way that allowed me to access their innocence.

What I appreciated the most about teaching at that small high school was the opportunity to be fully and completely me. Our principal hired one teacher who openly practiced Wicca, another teacher who was Buddhist, and another who was an atheist. We were mostly a young and passionate group of teachers who cared deeply about our subject matter and our students. The principal sets the tone of the school atmosphere, and that was an atmosphere of tolerance, love, and a dedication to the success of students.

The last six weeks of school for seniors in high school is usually a wash. Many of my students joined the military. Many also decided on a college, trade school, or beauty school. A few were close to delivering their first or second child, and I had to use creativity to hold their attention in some way.

I brought in my personal library, which included books like *Prozac Nation*, *Siddhartha*, *Tropic of Capricorn*, *Letters to a Young Poet*, *The Unbearable Lightness of Being*, *Beloved*, *Chocolat*, *A Woman's Worth*, *The Peaceful Warrior*, *The Tao of Pooh*, *Jitterbug Perfume*, *The Law of Success*, *The Liar's Club*, and *I Know Why the Caged Bird Sings.* Most of the students picked from my collection, but a few students picked biographies or books geared toward a scientific interest from the school library. Some students chose young adult novels, but they all wrote a review of their book. Then, we gathered in a circle and talked about issues in the books, issues in society, and issues in their own lives.

That last week of class before final exams was my favorite week with my seniors. The student who read *Prozac Nation* had never spoken up in class, but he passionately reviewed the book, talking about his own struggle with depression. By some odd twist of fate, he even had the same tattoo as Elizabeth Wurtzel—FTW (fuck the world), and showed us his tattoo. We laughed, but I felt happy that he was enthusiastic about the book because I wanted them all to enjoy reading. If I could inspire them to read with even a quarter of the enthusiasm that I felt for my subject matter, then I would have achieved my desire. Reading saved me from boredom and set my mind free as a child. Reading had also introduced me to various spiritual teachers while I stayed in bed in my body cast. I didn't know where their lives would take them, but I could only hope that that last project helped many of them develop a greater appreciation for reading.

I enjoyed each student's contribution to the class and they were engaged, which seemed like a miracle for seniors at the end of the year. There were many moments of happiness that flooded my being while teaching. As a student might answer a question or offer a moment from her life, I felt love from the other side pouring in to answer her. Many times, I believed that angels were all around me, occasionally talking through me for the benefit of these students.

That year, there were few absences except for senior skip day. I would miss these students, and believed they would always burn a little brighter in my memory because they were the first students in the U.S. that were mine for a full year, and we experienced 9/11 together.

While I graded papers like mad, I also stayed up until two, three, or four in the morning working on my own graduate work. The end of the school year gave me great peace because I had given the school year my best effort.

At my graduation, the president of Goddard College leaned in and whispered, "I expect great things from you."

He probably said this to most of the students, and I wondered if I had already done great things simply by caring deeply for my students. Several times that year, I knew that the greatness of the other side worked through me to connect with my students.

If nothing else, I knew that I gave my students kindness and some levity. I was never condescending or rude when they asked for my time. If they wanted my attention, they got my full attention. I might have been tired some days, but I felt genuinely happy to know each one of them.

Many NDErs feel that they have a mission once they return to Earth, but sometimes they are unclear what that mission might be. I got direct career guidance from God. Now, I realized that if I had avoided teaching, I would have missed some of the happiest moments of my life. God certainly knew me better than I knew myself. Anyone lucky enough to be in the zone—the flow, the space where information, communication, or a specific activity seems to flow effortlessly—knows the joy I felt so many times in the classroom. I could read the emotions of students, knowing when they zoned out, when ideas and connections happened in their brains, and when their hearts were moved. I could tell when they squinted in disbelief, so I pushed harder, breaking through their cognitive barriers. I felt the presence of my angels at times, taking over my body and giving me the right words at the right time.

I channeled for the benefit of my students and considered channeling as factual as eating. After all, I saw angels working through the doctors while they worked on my body. To experience these moments allowed me to feel divine love. Not every moment was channeled, and I certainly spent many nights doing the ordinary work of grading papers and preparing lecture notes.

The school year went by quickly, and every teacher loves the last day of school for the surprising thank you letters and heart-felt interactions. One of the football players required to rewrite his essay at the first of that year thanked me for preparing him for college. He had been so quiet and serious as he rewrote that first essay, paying careful attention to the formatting handouts and the review about plagiarism.

I remembered staring at the frosted bits of his hair that were growing out and wondered why that was in fashion for young men. Many of the students told me weeks before graduation about their plans, but he surprised me. He didn't ask for a letter of recommendation and got into a good state university, and he had serious, detailed plans for his future.

A young woman, who I was certain did not like me, told me that she was very bored by school, but I was one of her *least* boring teachers. She admitted to enjoying the book she read for her book report. Other notes landed on my desk, and a few of the more extroverted, gregarious students stopped by to say goodbye and tell me how much they would miss me.

Because I had such an amazing principal, I considered staying another year, but I also wanted to move out of Mom's house. I wanted the freedom to date and socialize more frequently. To live on my own and handle my student loans and other bills, I had to find a school district that paid a higher salary. Quickly, I found a public school in Dallas offering a decent salary. As I packed up my books, futon, and an inherited dresser, I knew that I would miss that high school and the slower pace of South Texas.

CHAPTER SEVENTEEN

RENEGADE

"You can't teach in a vacuum.
A good teacher relates the material to real
life. You understand that, don't you?"
—Frank McCourt, Teacher Man

I signed a contract with Dallas Independent School District for a junior honors class, but when I arrived at the high school for orientation, the chair of the department told me that I would be teaching ninth grade remedial English. She introduced me to fellow faculty members as, "This is Tricia. She has absolutely zero teaching experience."

I corrected her introductions, explaining my teaching experiences overseas, at boarding schools, and the senior English classes with one of the lowest drop-out rates in all the surrounding areas. I longed for my former administrators who spent long afternoons showing me how to be more involved in the lives of my students.

The school year at DISD did not start swimmingly to say the least. My second period class was ill equipped, and there were not enough chairs or books for my students. When I questioned the vice principal about the issue, she informed me that several of my students would be dropping out soon. The lack of respect and belief that this so-called teaching establishment showed toward its students was disheartening. I wanted a better environment for my students, not this toxic place. I wanted each of my students to feel welcomed and important, as opposed to feeling as if they were not worthy of textbooks and chairs.

Third period, a guy who showed up late decided that he didn't like being marked as tardy. His dislike turned to anger in the blink of an eye. And with menace painted on his face, he looked at me and said, "You know what? I'm going to kill you!"

"Go ahead," I found myself blurting out, surprising both him and myself. "I've made the worst decision of my life choosing to work here anyhow. The administration doesn't care about either one of us. I'm a near-death experiencer, so I'm not afraid of death. Go for it!"

He looked at me blankly for a moment, confused at the words that I had just thrown out at him. "Yeah…well I'm going to steal your hubcaps!" he said in a lame and ill-chosen flurry of words, all in an attempt to try and save face.

And true to his words, later that day, my flashy hubcaps were indeed stolen.

With overcrowded classrooms and teachers who were bullied and not supported by administration, I wondered how the students could endure these conditions long enough to graduate.

After two more weeks of demeaning treatment from my chair, I contacted my stepdad's cousin who worked as the superintendent. She wrote several letters for me in the hope that I might find a new position. After nine days of intense prayer, a junior high teacher in a small town south of Fort Worth left her position because of a complication with her pregnancy; the principal offered me the job. The salary would be the same as the small district I worked for near San Antonio, and I wondered how I would survive.

In those two final weeks at this high school, I felt more like a social worker than a teacher as I called CPS several times. The first time was for a fourteen-year-old girl named Michayla who came into my classroom agitated, angry, and chemically altered. Instead of sending her to the principal's office, which I knew was a joke, I moved Michayla's chair outside the classroom and told her that I would spend my off period with her. Since I promised to write her a note to get out of that class, she willingly stayed and talked with me.

When we walked around outdoors, Michayla broke into tears, telling me about her stepbrother who dealt cocaine. He introduced her to the drug and then forced her have sex with him once she became addicted. Now, she was pregnant and couldn't stop using the drugs he supplied. I was required to call CPS, but I wanted to talk with her first, devoid of all roles—just as a woman who cared about her.

To me, she looked like a little girl, and I cared deeply about her safety. I told her that I loved her and wanted her to feel that love. I told her that her life mattered more to me than any choices she made. I told her that God loved her deeply and explained to her how my time in the hospital allowed me to realize how much better my brain felt when it wasn't altered by drugs. I told her that I didn't judge myself for all that I had gone through. And that by that same token, I wasn't judging her either. I clearly understood that people often do drugs to escape the pain of their lives. I told her that her own health and life had to be her main priority and that she needed a ton of mothering and support herself. She needed therapy, a program of recovery, and a place to stay far away from her stepbrother.

I wasn't sure what CPS would be able to do for her, and I didn't know if her parents would prioritize her safety.

After talking for a while, I asked, "What do you want? Do you want to have this baby?"

Michayla looked at me somberly and fingered the cross nervously at her neck saying, "I might feel guilty, not sure, but I know that I hate my stepbrother."

I nodded and gave her the most common-sense advice I could give her. I talked for a long while, saying, "Michalya, you have a hard decision in the middle of a tough life situation. I could show you ten women who believe they made the best choice for themselves and their lives after having an abortion, and I could show you ten women who regret it and are haunted by their choice. I could show you ten other women who are both relieved and saddened by their choice, wishing that they had a different family or a different man in their lives at the time of their pregnancy. Each life experience is individual. Only you can know and experience your truth."

I went on to say, "The God I know from my near-death experience forgave me for everything that I had done, and did so instantly. God did not judge me and only wished that I had loved and taken better care of myself. God wants you to learn how to take care of yourself. I want you to learn how to take better care of yourself and to survive an unfair situation; honestly, it sounds like it is going to take Herculean efforts to save yourself in this family situation, much less save yourself and a child."

She stopped crying and said, "I have no idea how to take care of myself, or even how to make it."

Michayla looked so young to me, and I wanted to hug her. I didn't know what to say, but I replied, "I care about you more than any decision you might make. Even if I am the only person in this world who is saying this right now, please know that God is talking through me. You are loved. And, I know that you can make it through this time in your life."

Somehow, my love broke through her sadness, and I waited silently for her to speak. Eventually, she smiled and looked somewhat thoughtful and serene. We needed a bit of levity, so I found a picture of protesters at an abortion clinic on my blackberry. I pointed out how most of the protesters at abortion clinics were angry white males. She laughed when I said, "Are you really going to let these angry dudes make you feel guilty?"

Through a smile Michayla said, "Hell no! I bet if those guys could get pregnant, abortion pills would be given out in Pez dispensers."

I laughed at her humor and wanted to stay with her for longer than an hour. She was clearly in need of my attention. I was curious about what she wanted out of life beyond this moment and asked, "What kind of job would you like in the future?"

She thought for a moment and said, "I want to have a better life someday and maybe work in an office."

It made me sad that working in an office was her best idea of success. I wanted much more for her, so I told her, "All that and much more is possible."

I also let Michayla know that what her stepbrother did is considered statutory rape, but she said she felt guilty for wearing cut-off shorts around the house. I told her that a woman's body is her own, and she should be able to make choices about who can or cannot touch her. I told her that there would always be a lot of noise in society about how abortion is wrong, but these same people often don't care about low-income schools, low-income neighborhoods, or a culture that normalizes and rarely punishes assault on women and teens.

People will argue that adoption might have given that child a chance, but most of the same people who argue that are not lining up to adopt or foster minority children who are born addicted to cocaine. I was on the front line with this young woman, so I checked to see if my advice was in line with her highest good. The angels simply told me to remind her to take care of herself and love herself for all she would have to continue to survive. The thought of what she would have to continue to survive over the next few years saddened me.

When CPS showed up at her residence, her parents denied that the stepbrother had sex with Michayla. That told me all I needed to know about her family. A few days before my final day at this DISD high school, Michayla showed up at class. She was clean, sober, and no longer angry. She looked healthier than I had ever seen her. Michayla let me know that she miscarried, and I felt relieved that she didn't have to experience an abortion in addition to her horrific life situation. Her parents let her get on birth control, but she had to live in that situation. There didn't seem to be much practical help for teenagers, but I realized how the smallest bit of love and concern for someone could strengthen their survival skills.

I didn't want to leave my students, but I had zero faith in this crumbling school administration. I was honest with the students about their administration, their principals, my chair, and their lack of concern for students. On my last day of class, we had slam poetry events in each classroom, and I reminded them that we all deserved better treatment from this school district.

After leaving DISD, I wrote a letter to the *Dallas Morning News* and suggested they investigate this school. A few years later, DISD was in the news for problems with their superintendent. She was caught using school funds for cell phones for her family and other expenses. I imagined how this money might have been spent on books for my students.

* * *

In Fort Worth, I had to find a cheap place to rent quickly. I felt happy and a little terrified to live by myself—divorced, thirty, and existing on an unreasonably small salary. On faith, I found a small, affordable duplex near TCU and dove into the new school year.

My classroom sizes at the junior high were small, especially in comparison to DISD classrooms. My homeroom class consisted of eight students—seven boys and one girl suffering from a range of emotional issues. My goal was to get these eight students to calm down enough to read short stories in their textbook. One kid came to school after drinking an entire quart of soda. I didn't think he had emotional issues, but I informed him he was on his way to getting diabetes. I brought in articles about health, but they couldn't concentrate on anything long enough to read a paragraph, much less an article.

Knowing what I know about meditation, I brought in a CD to teach them how to breathe deeply and experience a few moments of peace. I hoped meditation might calm their agitated minds down long enough to focus on preparing for the up-coming standardized tests. Meditation worked far better than I imagined it would. A tall, sandy-haired boy looked up at the end of class period and said, "That's the first story that I've ever read from beginning to end. I can't believe it."

His obvious pleasure at his small achievement pleased me. After that, we spent the first ten to fifteen minutes of each class period trying different breathing exercises and a few guided meditations by Doctor Andrew Weil. I stuck with simple exercises that focused on simple yet powerful things like health and relaxation. I couldn't imagine that any parents would be upset.

Maybe they wouldn't have been if I had only used these exercises with my small homeroom group. Many of their parents were abusive or neglectful, and probably did not even ask their kids what they learned in school. However, when my homeroom students talked about the ten to fifteen minutes of meditation, the other classes begged to try it. For some reason, my honors class loved meditation most, often finishing their work quickly to have extra time for meditations.

Then, the Bibles started piling up on my desk from parents. One man with a handlebar mustache and clunky cowboy boots entered my classroom during an off period and quite simply said, "Ma'am, I'm a Christian. And I'd prefer my daughter's teachers be Christians too. Have you read this book?"

I sighed and crossed my arms, "Only a few dozen times," I replied.

He brightened a little and said, "Well good. I wouldn't want her to learn anything that counters the Bible."

Other student's parents sent Bibles with complaints to the effect of, "My child is not allowed to pray in class, so I would prefer that she not meditate in class." We did have moments of silence after saying the Pledge of Allegiance.

Students were welcome to pray silently during that time. Even when I attended church, most of the prayers spoken aloud seemed to be a pissing contest from various men, proving how godly they were. If my students hated meditation, they could simply rest, and I knew that a reduction in stress helped them perform better on tests.

When I received a psychotically angry letter from one mother who called me a devil worshipping heathen who was "corrupting her daughter" with Buddhism, I knew I would have to stop teaching mindfulness and meditation, even though the practice was greatly benefiting my students with emotional struggles. I wished I hadn't shared it with the other classes. The small original group was particularly sad to see me put away the CDs.

Unfortunately, the parents were not satisfied. They had a point to prove and a witch to burn. In 2003, mindfulness practices were not as common in schools as they are now—especially in a small town in Texas. Both my principal and superintendent asked for a copy of the guided meditations. The principal let me know that the matter had been moved up to the superintendent's office, and they would be contacting me. Since they had just lost a teacher because of a complicated pregnancy that required bed rest, I guessed that they weren't going to fire me. If I'm honest, I didn't really care if the school district didn't renew my contract.

Even if they fired me, I could probably have made more money waiting tables at a fine dining restaurant than teaching at that school. When I walked in, the superintendent appeared reasonable. He motioned me to sit in one of his maroon leather chairs and said, "Honestly, I listened to the entire CD and don't see what the fuss is all about, but because the parents made something so minor into such a big deal, you can't play this CD or teach mindfulness in your classroom. Okay?"

I nodded and said, "I understand, sir." I may be a subversive rebel at heart, but I treat authority with kindness, especially when they treat me with a bit of respect.

I listened to him as he talked about his time at this school district and his love for football. He was particularly irked that he didn't get to see the game because of all the parents who were pissed off that their kids were asked to meditate instead of praying.

I thought about saying, *"Isn't education about exposing people to things outside of their comfort zone?"*

I didn't though. Instead, I promised that I loved the kids and would stay under the radar for the rest of the year. He smiled at me and motioned me toward the door as his phone started ringing.

In the two years I stayed at this small junior high, I did—as promised—largely remain under the radar. But I did push my students to read things far more interesting and challenging than the practice tests for the standardized testing. I made them journal and taught them how to become more introspective.

I'll never forget one young man who wrote in his journal about how his parents were in the middle of a divorce and he felt that their divorce was his fault. I wrote back to him, encouraging him to talk with his parents about this. I told him that I was 100 percent certain that they would tell him his assessment of the situation was inaccurate. He stayed after class that next week and thanked me for encouraging him to talk with his parents. Of course, they assured him that he was not the cause of their divorce, but rather the greatest joy of their time together as a married couple. He went from being a young man who slouched in his chair and often looked on the verge of anger or tears to a more confident and self-assured person.

I thought about how my own high school English teacher had talked back to me in the journals I wrote in her class, challenging my limited views of my world and myself. Missus Platzer encouraged me to apply for scholarships and believe in myself. Her intervention into my life came at such a crucial time, often encouraging me to become more introspective and value the power of my mind.

I challenged a few of my students in similar ways, encouraging the young women to forget about the boys for a day and to focus on their own dreams and goals. I encouraged some of the young men to write about anything in their journals other than the movie *Jackass* or the video game *Grand Theft Auto*. I made all of my students write out five-year plans for their lives and positive visualizations.

During the week before a speaker came to talk with my eighth graders about abstinence, two of my girls told me about being molested. The counselor gave us a handout with startling statistics about this county and school. One in five students at this school reported sexual abuse. One morning, one of my sweet students completely broke down in class, and I sent her to counseling. Later that day at lunch, I heard some of the other teachers talking about how they didn't like the kids who wore Outkast and Lincoln Park T-shirts, insinuating that these students were wild and possibly "devil worshippers" for their music choice. I suggested that all kids deserved our support not judgment, and admitted to liking secular music myself. One of the science teachers continued expressing her views regarding sensitive topics. Earlier that year, this teacher overheard a student admit to the counselor that she had been raped at a high school party.

The teacher continued, "My son said that she wore a short, jean skirt to the party. I think she deserved to get raped for dressing like that in front of all those boys."

Although my jaw tightened, and I wanted to speak my mind, I calmly asked the name of the girl. I wanted to talk with her and help her in any way possible, especially to realize that victim shaming is wrong. It never made sense to me to blame the person to whom something is done rather than the person who did it.

I talked with this student, and her parents were aware of the situation and had talked with the police. The moment left her wise beyond her years. I told her that she is the one who deserves support, not the guys who raped her. She agreed with me and promised to look after others and talk openly about her story.

I didn't confront my fellow teacher right away, but I watched her. When she brought the topic up a second time, I firmly asked, "What if your son wore baggy pants to a party and passed out? What if a group of men gang raped him? Would it be his fault for wearing a tight white T-shirt that showed off his little pert nipples? Would it be his fault for exposing part of his boxers to men? Would you tell your son he was a little whore who deserved to be raped for wearing what he wore? Would you not call the police and blame him? Is that what you'd do if your son was raped, you stupid bitch?"

Her mouth dropped open. For once during lunch in the faculty lounge, she was completely silent and ate her lean cuisine quickly.

I took things too far with the vulgar language and wondered if she might report me to HR, but I didn't care. I also knew they wouldn't fire me with only a few months remaining in the year, and she deserved to have her hatefulness checked. Her outdated thinking irritated me, and I wanted to put an end to victim blaming. I wanted all people to support the rights of vulnerable teenagers, not shame them for being naïve. That hateful, puritan streak that runs through society needed to die. I was on the side of keeping young women and young men safe and helping them heal. I was on the side of angels, and I knew it. Even if my response could have been classier, I said what I needed to say.

That teacher left the lounge without saying a word, and one of the teachers who grew jalapeños in his backyard tried to break the tension by offering us all fresh jalapeños. I ate the jalapeño whole, even chewing the seeds. I barely felt my mouth burning for the rage. He pointed out that my face was redder after eating the jalapeño. "You're probably right," I replied and walked out of the lounge holding only the stem. Fire tasted good that day.

I didn't make any friends with my fellow teachers. I told a coach that it was creepy when he hugged the girls in long, full body hugs. I told a science teacher that a month on creationism was not going to help the students get into a good college or medical school. I didn't wear the T-shirts they wanted me to wear on game days, and I only stood for the Pledge of Allegiance once a week instead of every day because I had things to organize for class.

I ended my last year at that junior high school year with a bang, confronting bullies and insisting that the three guys demonstrating criminal behavior by chopping off the heads of buried cats with a lawnmower spend time talking with the counselor. I asked them to be responsible for saving the life of every bug trapped in my classroom. At the end of class, I made them set the dirt daubers, moths, flies, and hornets free, doing my best to teach them empathy. I also told them that I reported their names to the police and that they would stay on a watch list for any crimes against animals or people. I actually did call an officer who wrote down the three boys names and said he would talk to them and try to scare them.

When the rather odd, lanky speaker came to our junior high to talk about abstinence, I wondered if that talk mattered to the young woman who had been raped. Or to the young man who was raped by a pedophile in town. Many of the kids who suffered these traumas were sexually active. I certainly didn't believe that junior high was the appropriate age to become sexually active. Of course, abstinence makes sense, but in cases where students are already sexually active, sometimes because predators initiated them to sex, didn't they need information about safe sex?

Junior high couples did not need to bring babies into the world; rather, they needed emotional healing and education. Maybe with enough healing they might choose abstinence, but to leave out information about safe sex seemed foolish and even punishing to the students who were sexually active.

During the assembly, I could barely keep a straight face as the guy held up his hands and said, "See these hands. Look at these hands. These hands never touched my wife's breasts until we were married. I never touched her naked body until I wore a wedding ring."

This was the most awkward bragging session I had ever witnessed. His talk was out of touch and not heart-centered. After talking about how awesome he and his wife were for waiting until marriage to have sex, he jumped to fear tactics and showed the students pictures of various venereal diseases. He went straight from "I waited to have sex before marriage" to "these are the diseases you will get if you have sex before marriage."

Back in my classroom with a small group of students, I printed out articles that covered the type of talk given at schools that covered safe sex. I made it clear that abstinence was the best policy for their hearts, their immature minds, and their physical health. I also made it clear that I knew many students were already sexually active, and I did not think they would be great parents as a fourteen- or fifteen-year-old. They read the articles with interest, and one boy said, "I wish we had this talk at our school. It would have made a lot more sense."

All I could reply was, "I know."

There were kids who benefited from the abstinence-only talk, but there were also kids who needed a different kind of talk as well. I'm glad that I could be that different voice in their lives, a voice that cared about their physical, emotional, and intellectual growth. I wasn't there to judge them, but to ask them to consider how to live their lives wisely from a place of logic and balance.

That year ended beautifully, and I had never received so many open, heartfelt notes from students. During the last week of classes, I played chess with one of the more combative, rebellious student in my class. I barely beat him, earning his respect. One of the other troublemakers wrote a note saying, "I now see that you were only trying to make me a better person. You wanted me to succeed in life, to think deeper about my choices, and to grow up and be an honorable man. I treated you horribly and made fun of you, but you kept loving me and asking me to do my best. I see the truth now, and

I love you. Thank you for putting up with me and teaching me important lessons."

Although I might have broken down in tears at another time, I felt a bit annoyed that I had to put up with his disrespectful attitude all year only to see him "get it" the very last day. *At least*, I reasoned, *he eventually got it.* Not every junior high student can see that their actions and choices have consequences. He went from being a punk to a gentleman in a single day. The transformation was beautiful and reminded me that people do change and that teachers can play a vital role in helping students grow. By this time in my teaching career, I knew that God had clearly sent me back to cross paths with these young people.

CHAPTER EIGHTEEN

CROSSING OVER

"The truth will set you free.
But not until it is finished with you."
—David Foster Wallace, Infinite Jest

After working two years at the junior high, I transitioned into working as an adjunct professor at colleges in the Dallas area, and the flexible hours gave me more creative time. While working as a professor, I sent out several poems to various journals and magazines. Fortuitously, eight poems were published and acknowledged in various contests, and in the summer of 2007, I spent a month in St. Petersburg, Russia as part of the Summer Literary Series (SLS) program. International travel proved a wonderful antidote to the ups and mostly letdowns of my romantic relationships.

When I returned from Russia and a stopover in Paris for a few days, Dad called from the ER and told me he most likely had food poisoning. Something told me to get in my car immediately and go see him. I asked the heavens for answers about what to expect before I got to the hospital. As soon as

I asked, I saw a sign for a funeral home and my heart sank. I knew my dad would not be on the planet much longer.

When I arrived at the ER and grabbed Dad's big hand, the doctor on duty sent him for a CAT scan. Shortly afterwards, Dad was wheeled into a private room overlooking a garden in the same hospital where I was born. The doctor solemnly came in, turned off the television and said, "Danny, I have shocking news for you. You have a fast-growing brain tumor called Glioblastoma Multiform. Currently, it is the size of a grapefruit."

I burst into tears, and a few tears also leapt out of Dad's eyes. He quickly shook his head and said, "Stop crying, Tricia. I'm only crying because you are."

Then he joked, "You know, doctor, there are going to be a lot of people who are going to be happy once I have that stroke and can't talk anymore."

The ER doc replied, "Mister Barker, be serious. I'm giving you a death sentence, you realize. This means something to your daughter."

Dad nodded and smiled at me with love.

The ER doctor continued, "I'm going to have a neurosurgeon come in and talk to you shortly about possible surgery."

I didn't understand why the ER doctor was upset by Dad's humor. That's just who he was—an upbeat guy who could not be serious for more than forty-five seconds, but in those few moments of seriousness he assured me that he understood the diagnosis. Dad never cried again through the entire process. He signed over his life to me but held onto the wallet and keys for another hour, not wanting me to drive his car or to get the last ten dollars available on his credit card.

I particularly loved Dad's response to the pushy neurosurgeon who breezed into the room and barked out orders in a thick, Italian accent. I stepped outside with the surgeon and said, "I'm sorry, but my father has opted out of surgery."

The neurosurgeon, dressed up in an actual cape, replied, "Your father's tumor is pressing on the emotion sector of his brain. He can't be relied on to make decisions. You get to make the decision whether he has the surgery or not."

I bit my lip to stop the tears and replied, "I know my dad. He's had a lifelong fear of brain surgery because of what happened to his cousin after brain surgery. He knows he is going to die either way and prefers not to have the surgery."

I didn't tell the neurosurgeon that I couldn't take care of him after surgery anyway, but I couldn't—not in my studio apartment. The neurosurgeon was pissed, and turned away quickly, his cape literally flying out behind him. He yelled into my dad's room, "I won't be back if you change your mind."

My dad yelled loudly, "You might be a neurosurgeon, but you're not God."

The neurosurgeon guffawed and walked away.

I found a nursing home near my apartment in Dallas for Dad. We had grown closer once I became an adult. Though he wasn't around much when I was a kid, he was always good at giving unconditional love, and I wanted to return that love. I held his hand every night for the next month, giving him as much of my time as possible. Dad didn't take morphine because he wanted to be able to talk with me when I showed up after teaching classes. At first, he could still walk slowly, so we went outside on a bench and looked at the bright sunshine. When I asked him what he thought about this change in his life, he said, "Tricia, everything has a way of working out for the best."

I must have looked at him in horror, thinking the brain tumor was affecting his sanity. Things did not seem to be working out for the best in his case, and I wanted different circumstances for my father. I wanted him to win the lottery or hit it big at the track and share his fortune with me, or at least give me enough money to pay off my student loans. I wanted him to lose a few pounds, find a better job, and remarry. I didn't want him to die at sixty-three, alone in a nursing home, with only me and a few friends as his comfort and support. Most of all, I wanted more time with him.

That semester was one of the hardest teaching semesters of my life. I was scheduled to teach nine different college classes at three different campuses. Luckily, I could see Dad every evening and between classes. There were many days I ran out of class early, overwhelmed by loss but also grateful that I had experience with death and could help Dad by talking about my time in the afterlife. We talked about my near-death experience a few times, and he believed my stories of the light, assuring me that he had no fears about the dying process.

It turns out, I was the perfect guide to the other side for him, and he was exactly what I needed to reconnect with my spiritual journey. We laughed at death together and joked about how he deserved a marching band as he flew up into the sky to meet his maker. We blasted classical music, and ate greasy Chinese food, Doritos, ice cream, and whatever he wanted to eat before he could no longer eat anymore. We had about five days of "last meals." He reflected on some of the near misses and moments he might've died in Vietnam, telling me that he felt immortal back then.

Mom didn't plan on seeing Dad, but I asked her if she might reconsider as his conditioned worsened. Very quickly, Dad could no longer get out of bed. Mom visited him briefly, and I stood outside the door protectively, willing to step in if she wasn't kind. She proved sweet, saying, "Danny, you were always like a big wild cat that could never be tamed, but I did love you all those many years ago."

He laughed and said, "We did something right. We made her together."

Probably, he said this knowing I was on the other side of that door, wanting some closure between the two of them and the marriage I witnessed. Mom shared negative thoughts about Dad loquaciously. And, he said condescending things about her lack of intelligence, implying that at least he passed on a portion of his genius to me. I didn't think Dad with his greasy T-shirts with holes in the front could be much of a genius, even though he was wickedly funny and had a mind for facts.

A genius would have figured out how to live in a house nicer than a shack. A genius would have figured out how to get along with his wife or divorce her and find a more compatible wife. A genius would have seen that his daughter was hurting badly and been there for her. Dad was smart, but he wasn't a genius. He knew a lot about composers, artists in the Rococo period, and many historical dates. He would have made a good history professor or music teacher. His students would have laughed at his antics and learned a lot, but he chose to sell retread truck tires in East Texas. He sold just enough tires to have money for movies, weekends out of town, eating out, and paying bills.

Though Dad may not have lived his life well, he died fantastically well. We had over a month together, and I can't imagine a better performance at the end. When someone struggles desperately to live inside a dying body, it is a horrifying experience to watch. However, when someone winks at death, waves at it, grabs the conductor's baton out of death's hand and waves it around like he just doesn't care, you must laugh with him.

Dad laughed his way into heaven, and I don't think anyone could've died with more grace. Given the choice of a blissful meditation or laughing, I'll take laughing every time. Laughter is considered the best medicine, and my dad's final attempts at hilarity showed he was grateful to be alive, even in those last breaths.

When Dad was moved to hospice and the chaplain performed the last rites, Dad could barely lift his arm, but he made his best attempt to pretend to conduct an orchestra. The chaplain seemed a bit annoyed, but I realized that Dad was trying to make the moment lighter for me. He wanted me to remember his sense of humor and to show me how little he feared death.

After all, we came to Earth to laugh, to enjoy life, and to transmute this life into great healing, humor, music, or something beneficial or beautiful. Dad taught me that life is a grand adventure. He taught me to take risks even when they don't work out. Even though most of his life didn't work out that well, he gave me a great reserve of optimism, and in many ways, his optimism made perfect sense from a spiritual perspective.

I wondered if he might help me more on the other side than he did on this side and how clearly I would hear him once he transitioned. While in hospice, Dad could only squeeze my hand and look in my eyes. The day before he died, he did the exact same thing his father did before dying. Dad had a miraculous surge of energy and raised his hand in a farewell wave. That wave let me know it was okay to go home for a while and rest, and I swear that look made it more like an *I'll see you soon enough on the other side* kind of wave. I telepathically sent back a *Not that soon, old man.* He laughed without a sound, and as always, there was hilarity in the air around the two of us.

Dad's wave let me know that he was already in the hands of the divine, I could feel that his mother and father were there with him. For a moment, he even looked exactly like his father. Even in this seemingly unpleasant moment, a greater intelligence was easily perceivable to both of us. Dad recognized it, and I recognized it.

Around midnight I fell asleep and almost immediately had a dream where my grandparents talked with me in calming, comforting ways, hovering somewhere above the ceiling in spirit form. They told me that they were with Dad and had been with him for the last two days, waiting for him. They said they would instantly welcome him to the other side, would take loving care of him, and that I had done all I could for him. I woke up feeling more peaceful than I had felt in a while and looked down at my phone. I had three missed calls from hospice, and I realized what this meant. Though I wanted to be there at his time of Dad's passing, I felt comforted that his parents were with him. Their presence was warm and loving in the dream as it had been in life. I knew that he met the other side with curiosity, acceptance, and strength of spirit.

A few nights later, Dad came to me in a dream with the light behind him. He told me that he understood that I did all I could do within my time constraints. He assured me that he slept most of the hours I could not be with him so that he could be alert when I showed up. This relieved my guilt about how little time I had with him on some days.

Even though I was grieving, Dad's optimism was infectious, and he reminded me that any circumstance can be holy, any choice can be transformed into a better choice. He whispered to me that luck is indeed possible, and that we don't know all the answers, so it is better to trust the process. He also hoped that his passing might help me to forgive others quicker. I forgave him instantly when I realized he would be dying soon, and he wanted me to have more compassion and let go of pain from my past. He reminded me that love is all that matters, and in their broken ways, both of my parents tried to love me. Most of all, he wanted greater happiness for me.

Grieving the loss of my father proved difficult, so I threw myself into teaching, and I made sure that my students got involved locally and politically. Many of my writing assignments required students to contact various people in the community who could make a difference in our community. When some of my students received calls back from CEOs and the assistants of CEOs, they freaked out, worrying that they would not know what to say to someone in power. I spent a lot of afternoons and evenings coaching them on how to talk with business professionals.

Some of my students were from Nepal, Peru, or China; they feared their ability to communicate in English would not be strong enough to convince a CEO of a company to support a cause they cared about, but I encouraged them to consider this a learning experience. A few students had successful conversations with business owners, and their letters brought about a few changes at Brookhaven College. The president of the campus listened to their ideas and quickly installed recycling bins in each classroom.

More than any specific accomplishments in the classroom, I felt best when I simply connected with my students in informal and formal ways, letting them know I was there for their success. No matter the campus or course, I felt buoyant while teaching, knowing that God knew that teaching would give me joy and benefit others. However, I couldn't help missing Dad terribly. I wasn't sure that everything was working out for the best, but my life was certainly better than it might have been without a focus on helping others.

CHAPTER NINETEEN

HEALING

"Eventually you will come to understand that love heals everything, and love is all there is."
—Gary Zukav

Several months after Dad's death, he visited me in another powerful dream. It was hard to ascertain where he was, but it was clear that he was surrounded by love and communicating with love. I couldn't help but feel overjoyed to see him. Dad let me know that he had a lot to review and learn about the mortal life that he'd lived. He told me that because of this life review, he would not talk with me again like this, not for a while anyhow. He told me that he was in a state of spiritual evolution, and when he reached a place of greater understanding, he would contact me again. I wondered if the life-review that many near-death experiencers have is more extended when a soul goes there for a more extended stay.

Dad could feel the sadness I felt at hearing this, and with loving intelligence, he countered my sadness by explaining his process in the afterlife. Dad told me that he had to observe his life on what in our comprehension could be described as a virtual reality screen. And on that screen were several choices that he might have made in his mortal life. He could make each choice and observe how his mortal life would have turned out differently had he made each respective choice. Mostly, he had to review how his life might have turned out differently if he had lived closer to his potential. Fear, stagnation, and addictions limited some of his earthly choices.

To me, the process felt complex and somewhat disconcerting, but Dad put me at ease by telling me of the loving energy that was guiding him through the process, a loving energy that was teaching and loving him through the process. Dad always had a playful nature, and right now in a soulful state, that nature seemed amplified. He even made me smile when he dubbed this weighty and responsibility laden process as "Universe School."

I was happy again and felt at ease after talking with Dad, but it lasted for only a glimmering day or two and then a heavy sadness struck me. The realization that I wouldn't receive any dreams or messages from my dad for a while hurt. Food began to lose its taste, and I realized that this loss was something much worse than a breakup or divorce; this was no mere parting of ways. The loss of a parent is a profound loss, and one without compare. I am certain our very DNA understands the loss, and the grieving process has stages that cannot be skipped.

I kept Dad's phone on for a while, and I would call it to hear his voice on the recording; it was my audible memento of his unconditional love for me. His voice felt like both a beautiful yet cruel reminder, as I feared I would never have someone like him again in my life, someone to always be a champion for my side.

After a few more months had passed, Dad again came to me in another dream. I had waited so long to see him, and I was elated. Yet, in counter to my joy, he was concerned. He was worried about me and told me to focus more on my health. After that connection with him, I spent more time walking and meditating in nature. Dad's reminder was like a guiding light that helped me to find my way back to a vital lesson from my near-death experience.

We often neglect our connection to nature. In our technological age, we tend to be divorced from nature. Generations grow up with their faces glued to devices, and as a result find the feel and rhythms of nature to be alien to them. These generations miss out on the healing and calm that nature provides for humanity; one that is a key component to mental health. During my near-death experience, I was flooded with messages and one of them that resonated the clearest was that of reminding people to reconnect with nature.

Through a simple message from the afterlife, delivered first by angels and now by my dad, I decided to spend more time relaxing in parks or hiking. Memories seem to burn brighter in nature, as if the sunlight and world around us help to make the moments we spend in nature more powerful. I also realized that my stress level and depression decreased after spending time in nature. Even sitting on my balcony and watching the large oak trees brought me greater peace. Nature brings us more balance and harmony because it *is* balance and harmony.

Many people who experience a spiritual awakening have a greater awareness of the energy of certain foods and the importance of treating our bodies like temples. I committed to the change of treating my body much like I did during those first few years after my near-death experience when I focused my eating largely on organic fruits and vegetables.

I also learned how to address my anxiety and PTSD without prescription medications. Over the years, I had received a couple of long, rambling emails from Dave, the frightening man who sent the package to South Korea. Dave informed me in an email that he moved across the country and lived a few towns away from me. His website listed five or six women he had "lost contact with" over the years. I prayed for these women, imaging that he might have terrified them into hiding. Hearing from him rattled me, but I didn't want the energy of a sick person to take away my life force energy. I documented what I could document and made a vow to speak publicly about stalking and rape at some point in my future.

Mostly, I longed to be free of post-traumatic symptoms associated with trauma. I talked with my doctor about tapering down on my Ativan usage and switched to St. John's Wort, a natural antidepressant. The process was initially horrible, but I was prepared to make this change. Throughout the nights of panic, I sent love to my frightened heart, imagining all my stored fears finally leaving my body. Eventually, I began to sleep without fear.

During this time, I also listened to inspirational speakers and worked on changing my thinking patterns, consciously working on developing a more positive mindset. It was easy to uplift others, but I didn't extend this same grace to myself, at least not frequently. I confronted the negativity about myself that swirled around in my thoughts daily. The movie *What the Bleep Do We Know* was released a few years prior, and I rented it, thinking for a long while about the main character, Amanda, and how her life changed with a different, more uplifting mental focus. There is much more to the process of changing one's life than developing a positive outlook, but sometimes that positive outlook gives a person the energy to work harder and reach for a better life.

My focus was attuned to my healing, and I realized that the greatest aspect of my journey would reside within self-love. I consciously worked on shifting my attention from wounds, abuse, or disappointments in my life and instead placed my focus on the love I that experienced during my near-death experience and devoted time to incorporating more unconditional love into my life.

My connection to the other side continued to strengthen, but what probably aided me the most was my intent to be open to those divine channels of healing. In the presence of God's love, I also knew how to love myself. Back on the earth plane, this proved more challenging, but I reached out to others for help. A variety of healing modalities interested me, and I tried everything from shamanic healing to hypnotherapy. Any modality specializing in the release of trauma called to me.

I invested in massages, acupuncture, PSYCH-K, rapid eye movement therapy, craniosacral therapy, lymphatic therapy, hypnotherapy, and yoga. I went to see functional doctors and various energy workers. Part of healing from complex trauma comes from learning to create and cultivate harmony in one's life, often in new and peaceful ways. I created as many peaceful memories as possible and felt the angels offering their support as they had during surgery.

After my dad's death, I also actively sought a full-time teaching position at the community college level, applying to community colleges in Arizona, California, Georgia, and Virginia. Although I dreamed of getting out of Texas, I also applied in Austin, Dallas, and Fort Worth. Years before, I heard about the plans for a downtown community college campus in Fort Worth, and I experienced a quick vision that I would work there.

My last semester at Brookhaven College, I had a following of students from Nepal, sweet young men and women who worked at restaurants near the college. I stayed after class helping them outline possibilities for their essays. They put their trust in me since I had experience teaching English overseas in

South Korea. I understood their struggles with the language, and they worked hard and asked a lot of questions after class.

One pair of siblings even gave me their home address in Nepal and told me I was welcome to visit and hike through some of the beautiful forests near their homes. They said their parents appreciated my kindness, and I felt connected to these parents in a far-away land, if only for a moment in time. I wished I had the money to visit, but I barely had enough money for all the supplements, treatments, and organic groceries that I required. My new focus on health didn't come cheaply, but I knew it was vital. This realization kept me whole and balanced during my job search, resolutely staying true to my vision of healing myself and creating a light-filled future. I felt complete in the classroom and aware of divinity working through me as I reached out to students who were hurting, struggling, or just lonely and lost.

In late spring and early summer, I interviewed with committees and deans in Flagstaff and San Diego. I drove to Austin twice for interviews. I met with administrators at Brookhaven, El Centro, and Trinity River Campus. Even though I longed to leave Texas, I fell in love with the administration at Trinity River Campus.

And as fate would have it, I landed that job at the Trinity River Campus in Fort Worth, Texas, a beautiful campus fashioned from Radio Shack's headquarters with classrooms that overlooked a flowing river, much like the one from my near-death experience.

I had never been a part of the energy needed to open a new campus, and I loved the experience. Doctor Fulkerson, our president, championed every one of our causes to help promote student success. She cared about all the souls who flowed into our campus, and I knew that her good energy would be a huge part of the success of the campus.

In the classroom, I forgot about everything except my students, knowing that God has a way of choosing wounded healers to work miracles. At Trinity River, I worked with homeless students, returning military veterans, women fleeing violent marriages, students battling mental illnesses and physical illnesses, and thousands of first generation college students, as well as plenty of traditional community college students returning to college or entering after high school to pick up credits before university. I cared about every student who entered my classroom, and I'm sure that my students knew this on some energetic level.

Students were very excited about our gorgeous campus, and we often received compliments about how accessible we all were to the students from the top level down. Our campus president, Doctor Fulkerson, walked students to their classes when they were lost, and students often commented on how rare it was to even meet a campus president, much less be granted her full attention.

Doctor Fulkerson asked us to champion our students' successes and to quell their fears, and one of the best books I read on this subject matter was *The College Fear Factor* by Rebecca Cox. This book showed how students and instructors commonly misunderstand one another. The research that showed how anxiety can negatively affect student performance, so I began to include lessons about visualizing success and dispelling anxiety. Fostering student success was an easy mission for me because I wanted nothing more than to build my students' self-esteem and celebrate their accomplishments.

Doctor Fulkerson led our campus with her heart, and we couldn't help but follow her leadership. In many areas, our campus quickly became a model for other campuses in the district. God orchestrated this job for me, and as I helped add healing to the lives of students my own healing deepened.

CHAPTER TWENTY

THE RIVER FROM MY NEAR-DEATH EXPERIENCE

"He makes me lie down in green pastures;
He leads me beside quiet waters. He restores my soul;
He guides me in the paths of righteousness...."
—Psalms 23:2–3

Early that first year of teaching at Trinity River Campus, I remembered the vision I had during my near-death experience right before I was told to return to my body and teach. I knew that Trinity River Campus was part of God's mission for me. During my near-death experience I knew that I should remind souls of their light and potential in this world, so I found a way to weave my near-death experience story into many of my lectures. When a classroom overlooked The Trinity River, I asked the students to consider spending time walking along the river when they were stressed or tired.

The first two women who approached me after hearing about my near-death experience had lost very young children, and their hearts seemed to cry out for the reassurance I could provide them that their babies were surrounded by love. One woman researched grief and resources for healing for her final research paper. The other woman wrote lovely poetry to memorialize her son, and I thanked the heavens for my small part on their journey, hoping that my story offered some comfort to the women.

Each semester at Trinity River, I took groups of students outdoors to give them an experience of meditation in nature, and faces seemed more relaxed and happier, even after a short meditation outdoors. Though some of the student might've thought that the activity was a waste of time or a way to get out of lecture, time spent in nature was a focus on their health and divinity.

The first three years of teaching at a new campus flew by quickly. During awards ceremonies, I often felt stunned to see how far some students progressed. One student talked openly about how he only attended community college because a judge suggested that this would be his last chance to straighten out his life. He talked about how every class he took at Trinity River Campus showed him a future that he never had imagined for himself, a future in academics that he now embraced. He went from being a troubled young man to a student with a perfect grade point average and a future as an educator. Education saved me, and I knew it had the power to save others. I thought about the students I taught in high school who were involved in gang activities, and realized I was on the other side of that experience, helping some of those types of students who wanted a better life.

At graduation ceremonies, I prayed that my students would find careers that would best suit their personalities, creativity, and talents. God promised that my light would be a light that helped turn on their lights. I eventually realized that this meant that I could turn away from my past, turn away from everything that had happened before the wreck, and intimately know the love of God. I could bring this love into my life at any time, and I could remind others, in indirect and direct ways, that they too could be filled with this love for themselves and others.

After a few years at TCC, I witnessed many of my prayers for students get answered. Several single moms got full scholarships to large universities and landed good-paying jobs that allowed them to take their children on vacations for the first time. I saw many young men who made mistakes in their youth land professional jobs. Many of my students from those early years at TCC thrived and succeeded, moving on to larger universities; a piece of my heart followed them on their journeys.

Like teaching at the high school level, I still encountered students who were hurting intensely. I taught a beautiful young woman whom I will call Rose who showed up high for my creative writing class. When I confronted her about her drug use, she told me about the abuse she survived and how she started using coke and meth in high school. A teacher had intervened back then and contacted her mother. Her mother and father were divorced, and when her mother heard about the abuse Rose's father had inflicted on their daughter, she only asked that Rose's father pay for her counseling. I let Rose know that her mother should have pressed charges against him and that he should not be allowed around his other children.

That afternoon, I walked Rose down to our counseling center, and I told her to make herself and her healing her highest priority. A few weeks later, Rose passed out at her place of work and was diagnosed with a brain tumor, luckily not the fast-growing kind. She survived surgery, returned to class sooner than I imagined possible, and read two of her lovely poems at my open mike event. She let me know that she had also gone to rehab after surgery to deal with her addictions. I loved seeing young students understand the importance of recovery from drugs and alcohol quicker than many people of my generation learned this lesson.

Not all my interactions with students were intense or personal. I had many brief, happy connections, often writing letters of recommendation for them. Many of my students who celebrated graduation wildly were the first person in their family to get a college degree. I worked with countless others who worked full time, had families, or had health issues but also had the courage to keep working toward a better future. I believe in the power of education. I believe that my love, however small its contribution, sent my students out into the world with more confidence.

Service to others is one of the greatest gifts we can give ourselves. Connection is vitally important and giving of myself to my students proved the most joyful experiences of my life. It didn't matter if I woke up and felt depressed, disheartened, and traumatized by memories of my past. It didn't matter if I felt burdened by financial or romantic relationship difficulties. My problems simply didn't matter. What mattered is that I showed up willing to help others.

I listened to their stories of battling depression, their stories of heartbreak, and their stories of trauma. I pointed them to the right resources and in directions that might help them.

When a young woman told me about her experience with date rape in her past, I shared that piece of my journey with her and suggested that she commit to recovery with a strong healing focus. Sometimes, simply being present with someone and listening to them is a deeply healing activity. We did that for each other that day, and I understood that God could take my worst experiences and make these experiences beneficial to my students. Love is indeed all that matters.

On many days after teaching, I hung out with my students and listened to their hopes for their futures. Often, I wanted to say, "If I can do this, I know you can do this." Since trauma had not destroyed me, my life itself was a form of victory. I knew that many of my students understood exactly what I was trying to teach them. I knew that if I could survive my childhood and get through college battling depression, they could too and maybe even find a way to healing quicker than I did.

If I could start a graduate program, despite a violent ex-husband, they could get through college and transcend their circumstances. If I could wake up with enormous pain in my body and stand before them with great hope, joy, and enthusiasm, they could show up for class despite their struggles. We could make it together. I was certain about this much. I gave them the benefit of the doubt. I gave them my prayers and begged my angels and their angels to work for their good.

At Trinity River Campus, I quickly experienced popularity as an instructor, and my courses filled up as soon as registration opened. Each semester I got the chance to mentor at least a couple of students, and these mentorship experiences felt more like friendships. There was so much laughter during service learning events, even cleaning up trash on the river together proved fun. Nothing could have brought me as much joy as the moments I spent talking with students, and I knew that my success was also the success of God's love for these students.

The students at Trinity River were also fortunate to be a part of those magical first five years; in fact, our campus even had a magical mission dubbed "the Disney method" based on the book *Inside the Magic Kingdom: Seven Keys to Disney's Success*. Everyone from the enrollment department to the janitors tried to make a difference in these students' lives. During those first five years, the faculty formed learning communities, participated in service learning with students, and made ourselves available to mentor students and be there to help them succeed.

My career brought me so much fulfillment that I planned on teaching for TCC until retirement. After all, the light left me with no other message other than return and teach. At the end of my fifth year at Trinity River Campus on an ordinary day when I walked up the steps to my fourth-floor office after grabbing a salad in the cafeteria, I heard a loud, booming voice that seemed to ring from deep inside of me and far outside of me say, "Your mission is completed. You can stay and teach if you want, but you can do what you want with your life now."

Even though I am open to messages from my angels and messages from my dad or someone else's loved one, I nearly dropped my salad on the floor when I heard this undeniable voice. This powerful moment felt as if God had stepped in once again and altered my path. I had no plans to do anything other than teach for the rest of my life.

After a year or two of stunned confusion, I eventually realized that I wanted to write this book. My body would only be here for however long it is meant to be here, but my soul yearned to touch the hearts of people around the world and to let them know that we are deeply loved by God. I wanted to share what I had learned from living out God's mission for me and why a life of service and connection to others is a beautiful way to live. Sure, all the modalities and focus on health was important in my life, but I attribute my greatest moments of healing to being needed by other human beings and filling a void in their life with love. Beyond the words on a page, I wanted to pass on the energy of love.

All of us have access to an unlimited supply of love, and I wanted others to know that no matter how difficult their lives might currently be, they are loved immensely and can do magnificent work in the world if they can open themselves up to healing, love, and kindness. We are not only loved completely, but we are an actual extension of that love of God.

During those first five years at Trinity River, my career dominated my life, and my personal journey largely remained a healing journey. One afternoon, I realized on a deep level that I only needed to return to what I had known since I was twenty-two and encased in a body cast and deeply in touch the wisdom of the other side.

The lessons from the near-death experience contain timeless truths. Love is what matters most, and God is a force of great love. We are intrinsically and deeply connected to this powerful divine light, and it is our divine right to love ourselves the way God loves us. One of the most important things we can do on the Earth plane is to not harm others. If there is any way that we can help others or spread kindness, this is what we should seek to be of service to others. And, when we are lost or wounded, time in nature, prayer, or meditation can bring us greater peace.

Though I consciously chose not to have kids of my own, I have looked at my students—all of them—-as if I am substitute parent for a few hours, even when I am younger than them. If in some way I could increase their self-esteem, teach them a specific skill, or guide them in a solid direction, then I knew I had done my job. People do not get enough unconditional appreciation in their lives, so I gave them my complete attention and presence.

* * *

Profound personal healing, for me, happened in random places—a healing cathedral outside of Santa Fe called El Santuario de Chimayó. The cathedral is small, but the energy of the place is intense and filled with heart-centered love. Most people spend several moments in prayer and light a candle for themselves or a loved one. Then, visitors enter a tiny room to gather some of the healing dirt to take home. The walls outside the tiny room with the hole in the ground are lined with pictures of people who experienced instant healings and those that family members still hold in prayer.

During my first visit there, I asked for healing from neck pain. Instead, while praying in the cathedral, I experienced an amazing moment of healing that washed away wounds from childhood. I felt the presence of Jesus beside me, reminding me of his love for me. I remembered the message in the afterlife to "be like a little child," and I thought of how that message must have been from Jesus, even though I didn't see his form in the afterlife. As a child, I had a pure faith that opened the doors to heaven.

I was shocked and surprised to feel Jesus because for so long, I had not cared much for Christianity. The abuse I suffered as a child stood between me and that portion of the light that comes through Christianity. I felt some of my innocence return that day, and everything that I connected to Christianity in a negative sense was washed away by his loving presence.

In that moment in the cathedral, I became like the child the light had asked me to be. Healing passed from the conscious level to the subconscious, and I felt opened like a flower to receive more of the light from the other side. I also felt the beginning of true forgiveness for everyone, not for their sake but so that I might be free. The end of suffering is accepting things as they are without wishing for a different past or outcome.

A few years later, I went back to El Santuario de Chimayó with the same hope of finding an answer for my neck pain. I had exhausted traditional medical methods for my neck issues, racking up huge bills for MRIs and specialists. I had tried acupuncture, Rolfing, massage, yoga, core strengthening, energy healers, and traditional chiropractors. However, nothing diminished the pain for more than a few hours or a couple of days. A day after visiting the cathedral, I tried a session with a NUCCA chiropractor. When I walked out of my first session, I felt enormous relief from pain, and my body was in complete, happy shock. I sat on a park bench in stunned silence giving thanks to God.

I had been living with what I would call an eight or nine level of pain that radiated from my neck and head into my mid-back or lower back on occasion. My spine felt like it was on fire, like a snake's fangs were constantly biting into the back of my neck. It was hard to concentrate, sit, and grade the hundreds of essays I needed to grade. My campus purchased a standing station for me which helped quite a bit, but pain was a constant. For so long, I pushed away thoughts of physical pain, grateful simply to be alive and be able to walk but there were many days that I wished I might be able to shuffle off this mortal coil and merge with the divine love waiting for me.

Many people did not understand my chronic pain, especially the man I was in a long-term relationship with who often told me that I appeared to be the epitome of health; however, looks can be deceiving. Even when he rested his muscular forearm over my shoulder, I felt indescribable pain, and I felt sad that I couldn't enjoy something as simple as having my partner's arm resting on my shoulder.

Certainly, people face more difficult physical issues than me, but I am aware that a major injury like I had in 1994 has a price. I am somewhat fanatical about my diet, and eat to live the best possible life I can live, still largely focusing on raw organic fruits and vegetables. NUCCA sessions relieve pain for several weeks at a time, and that is as close to a miracle as I could imagine.

On the third visit to El Santuario de Chimayó, I spent a long time there, wondering why this place meant so much to me. I wondered why I had been given a message that I didn't have to teach anymore, and I wanted an answer. Instead, while in the cathedral, I felt greater self-control. I felt more peace, security, and fulfilment, no matter how my life turned out. I felt incredible gratitude for not having died at twenty-one as a depressed, lost young woman in college, doing her best to make it to the next level of success in the world but failing to love herself. I looked back at that young girl and wanted to hold her in my arms and tell her that I would be there in the future to help her.

We can either hate our life situations or fully embrace them in the light. I chose to embrace every situation and bring these situations into the light. I survived everything I survived, and I realized with certainty that I can use what I have learned to help others. As I reflected on my life in the cathedral, the completeness of this moment pleased me. I sat back in the pew and smiled—I largely and miraculously felt healed.

On my journey, I continued to work on embracing freedom over fear. I learned new coping skills and worked to release the pain of situations so much quicker than I ever imagined possible. One afternoon, I simply got over a painful situation after exactly five minutes of intense, fully present crying in my car. I asked God to come into my life and heal my heart and mind. This light immediately poured in, and I laughed at how easy it was to let go of that situation.

Part of healing was learning how to comfort my inner child and how to parent her. A child believes the world will take care of her with deep and abiding faith, so I had to shift into feeling worthy of the love and abundance I know exists in the presence of God. I connected with my innocence, optimism, and forgiving nature.

When I think of my inner child, I imagine the child I once was in the country—a child who prayed wholeheartedly and believed her life had divine purpose from the first moment she looked at the stars and the space between the stars. I picture my inner child as the child I never had, and I know that the darkness of the world might throw ridiculous moments at her, but her heart will grow stronger. I remind her that she deserved a much better childhood and that I can give her that now. I will not let her stay in situations where she might be abused or harmed. I will manifest many moments of immense joy for her, and shower her with kindness.

My inner child loves to laugh and dance under the stars. She sends her wishes to the moon when it is full, and watches those wishes magically descend into her life. She has intellectual breakthroughs and finds peace and healing in the embrace of nature. She is amused by creative, fun moments. She feels the love and healing energy of angels, archangels, ancestors, and guides. They work through her to help others realize greater levels of their spiritual power and connection to God.

She loves deeply, and she is deeply loved in return. The part of her inner child that is in touch with the light will never die. Her purpose will become more focused and her goals will take her places; these places will be filled with light and joy. And the vision she saw of herself as a very young girl will be closer to the truth than she realized.

She imagined herself growing up to become a sorcerer, one whose face looked younger than her years. She saw herself standing in her own power, and sending light into the world; all in a mixture of transcendental meditation and love for all living beings. Even if no one knew of her peaceful wishes for humanity, she would continue to go out to her backyard to pray for the freedom of every tortured soul on earth.

She would pray that everyone's relationships were filled with joy and ease. And that all people had access to healthy food and unpolluted waters. She would do what she could and donate as much as possible to help humanity. Most of all, her consciousness would guide others to greater healing and greater inner freedom. She would know that her own healing and the healing of others comes from the divine light of the universe. She would know herself as more light than anything else, a light that disintegrates attacks and soothes every wound.

I see the present me and the future me both sending love back to that child standing alone in the middle of a grassy field near a bale of hay. I am her true mother and grandmother, whispering of hope and a path that leads to great beauty. I send her love and peace from the stars as she gazes at them. I whisper to the young child that she will find her way through life and find her way back to the light of the divine. An immense amount of love waits for us and wants to embrace us all.

EPILOGUE

"Joy is the serious business of heaven."
—C.S. Lewis

Endings seem like beginnings, and beginnings seem to be continuations. From the perspective of the other side, time is perceived differently, and it's easier to see that our mortal lives are short. This knowledge has reminded me to deeply enjoy and accept the moments in my life.

Existence is, at the core and essence, pure love. Being in the presence of God was the most powerful part of my near-death experience. No matter how treacherous my journey became after that moment, I could never forget the love of God. Even when that love of God was only a pinpoint far in the distance, I knew that I am loved, and I am the light.

The consciousness I knew outside of my body was expansive, infinite, and beautiful. I realized that as I returned to my body, all that consciousness would be pushed through and filtered through my brain and set of experiences, and this seemed disappointing. Death was a gift—a gift of wisdom and a new perspective. That connection to love and source is everything. In fact, nothing matters more than a connection to the love and the knowing beyond what we know. Nothing matters more than knowing that we are loved by God.

Outside of physical form I felt freedom—the freedom to feel perfect as I am, the freedom to fly without fear, the freedom to let go of the imprisonment of negative thinking and the painful judgment of others.

There is a reason God reminded me to be like a little child and to remind others to go to nature for healing. As a culture, we are in desperate need of innocence, play, and healing. Most of all, every one of us needs more unconditional love because unconditional love has the power to heal us and to grant us greater acceptance and ease.

One of the most important things I have learned from dying is that death is not real but feels like birth into a new realm of understanding. We go on, and we keep learning and exploring. We continue to understand our connection to God and how deeply we are loved.

One important thing I have learned from communications with my father and others in the afterlife is not to focus too much attention on our little world when it is minuscule in comparison to the universe. Focus on being kind and loving, but don't overestimate your importance or influence in the vast expanse of the universe. We all, even the smartest and most spiritually advanced, know very little.

In other words, it is best to leave the specifics to God and to continue to find wonder and awe in the experience of being alive and connected to infinite bliss. The more you remember to connect with infinite love, the happier you will be on the roads and paths of your life.

The more I remember to connect with this love and bring this light into my life, the happier I am. Ultimately, I hope that you might bring this light into your life frequently.

If you are in a painful relationship, bring in the peace of God. If you are ill, bring in the light like a flood of great happiness. If you are fearful of the next steps of your journey, embrace the light and open yourself to immense freedom of spirit. Whatever your life situation, bring in more light and love and watch your world and the worlds of others collide and brighten.

Never be embarrassed or ashamed of your struggles. In the end, hardships are not a progress-stopping disadvantage. Many times, disadvantages become our greatest assets because the strength of our spirit prevails. When we create victory out of misfortune, we prove how powerful and resilient we truly are. God can work through us in many ways.

When we learn to breathe through pain, and how to keep walking toward the sunlight of our life and dreams, we prove true the divinity that resides within us. And by doing so, we free others to be stronger and to walk through all they must walk through in their lives.

And when you need extra help, there is no shame in reaching out to others. Look for the counselor, minister, healer, or life coach who can step aside from his or her ego and be a channel of the unconditional love of God. The modality that someone uses as a healer is not as important as the amount of the unconditional love of God these healers are able to bring to those in need. Many people are awakening to their own gifts on intuition and healing, and honest healers know this and help others find their own sense of power. Love is an energy that allows you to be reminded of how to connect with your own joy and connection to source.

Angels often appear in near-death experiences because they provide healing and guidance to souls in transition out of form as well as a connection to divinity. I hope that my knowledge of angels and healing helps readers to call upon their own angels and guides to help them navigate difficult patches in life.

By showing my trials and tribulations and how I worked to overcome them, my ultimate wish is that my readers will gain both solace and inspiration. And that they may take these gifts and trade them for the hope that incredible moments of healing and power await them in their own lives too.

You can live with more joy and freedom than you currently can imagine possible. Remind yourself of the descriptions of near-death experiencers near the presence of God. This is our natural state and how we should feel throughout our lives. It is easy to get thrown off-balance, but remembering our divinity allows us to thrive. I'm not overwhelmed by my past. I deeply enjoy the gift of this life—the magic of being, the magic of knowing that there is more to existence than the enjoyment the five senses provide.

At many times on my journey, I longed to feel safer and thought safety might come from romantic love. In my experience, safety didn't come that way. Though romantic love can be a deep source of connection to the divine, others cannot fix us, nor can we save them. Healing came from loving myself and giving love to the world. Healing came through faith in my divine purpose and not fighting that purpose. Healing came from acceptance, but also envisioning a bright future and believing unwaveringly in that future. A loving partnership is a blessing, but a relationship is not a substitute for God or for healing work.

Even though I had much to recover from in life, the near-death experience allowed much greater love and light into my life. Joy, hope, and beauty multiplied in my life when I stayed focused on teaching. Many days after teaching classes,

I rested in a hammock, looking up at the birds, squirrels, and sky, knowing that everything was right in my world. Much of that joy comes from being of service to others. The more I am in motion, asking how I might help others, the more my own pain is lifted away.

Even writing does this because writing about trauma releases it at even deeper levels and forces greater healing through the body, mind, and soul. Complex trauma is part of my story, and it is my hope that others might more fully commit to the long but worthy journey of healing. Sometimes, healing is cumulative, and in a single moment, it is simply possible to feel freer and better. Much like a near-death experience, a spiritual healing or transformation can occur seemingly instantly.

The trauma and loss I have survived has connected me to many students in need of my support. If students needed to talk about surviving child abuse, rape, stalking, domestic violence, depression, suicidal ideation or any combination of these issues, they picked the right person to talk with about their circumstances. If they were in an abusive relationship, I gave them the statistics I wish my counselors might have given me and warned me not to continue down that road with him. I directed them to memoirs like *Crazy Love* by Leslie Morgan Steiner and to various crisis centers and counselors at our school.

I have courage now, and I don't run away from pain. I feel it, walk through it, and release it. Feeling the pain and all the places that I have been shattered allows for more wisdom to come through me. However, like any inexperienced shapeshifter, any caterpillar who has become a butterfly, any phoenix rising from the ashes, the reality of flying through life and creating dreams takes practice.

More love than I ever imagined possible greeted me on the other side of this life, and I also know this love is available to us all while we live our lives, not just in death. This knowledge should give us all great inner freedom.

I believe in your journey as much as I believe in my own. So, take my belief in you and multiply it. Multiply it by adding to it, your own belief in yourself. You may not see the love of God, and the angels may escape your perception, yet they are there. Their presence is undeniable, and they walk with you. Know this and know that you are never alone. The angels from the OR are realer to me than any reality in my physical existence.

Understand that the healing that you seek, from whatever wounds you have suffered, resides within your next decision. For healing through the divine is only a small, easy, natural decision to open your heart and mind to more love. And, remember, much of healing is common sense. Whatever it takes to get to a place of eating healthier, dealing with addictive behaviors, and finding more inner peace, then make those choices immediately.

I pray that you will decide to embrace the beauty of both your mortal and eternal life, and that you will let this beauty shine forth a light upon your existence; one that fills your mind, body, and soul. You deserve all this and much more.

May you be blessed with love.

ACKNOWLEDGMENTS

I want to thank Chris Brethwaite, longtime Hallmark writer and former chapter head of Kansas City IANDS (The International Association for Near-Death Studies), for reading the early versions of my manuscript. I appreciate his encouragement, conversations about near-death experiences, and painstaking edits of my manuscript. Chris is also working with me on a screenplay adaptation of this book.

The writing process was a joyful one because of the developmental editing ideas of Matthew Limpede, the Executive Editor of *Carve Magazine*. Matthew Limpede worked diligently on my manuscript, and his feedback was invaluable. I also appreciate the beautiful editing and revision suggestions of key chapters from Kara Post-Kennedy, Ethan Michael Carter, Charli Mills, and Dennis Wayne Radcliffe. I am thankful for the former students and fellow faculty members who met me for creative writing groups after long days at the campus. I especially appreciate the feedback from my talented colleagues Dr. Terri Schantz and Shawn Stewart.

I am eternally grateful to my literary agent Jill Kramer at Waterside Productions who was the former Editorial Director at Hay House, Inc. Her advice and support meant a lot to me on this journey. I have thoroughly enjoyed working with Debra Englander at Post Hill Press.

My memoir, *Angels in the OR: What Dying Taught Me About Healing, Survival, and Transformation*, ends on a graceful note because of my wonderful teaching position at Tarrant County College and for the leadership of Dr. Tahita Fulkerson, our former campus president. Her focus on student success and community outreach meant the world to me as a near-death experiencer.

As a near-death experiencer, I am grateful for Dr. Jan Holden's research and for her introduction to the producers for The Biography Channel. My NDE story was profiled in the first season of *I Survived Beyond and Back*. Dr. Holden connected me to journalists for *National Geographic* and *The Atlantic*.

I would like to thank Diane Nichols, author of *God Gave Me You*, who covered my story in Simple Grace magazine. Also, Silvia Isachsen, who runs Angel Biz Academy, helped me launch The First Annual Online Near-Death Experience Summit. Silvia's marketing expertise and friendship helped me tremendously on my journey. I'm thankful for the engaging interviews with Janneke Øinæs from Wisdom from North, Sandra Champlain from We Don't Die Radio, Karl Fink from Streaming for the Soul, Lee Witting from NDE Radio, and Lisa Jones, The Millionaire Medium.

I appreciate the support, endorsements, and friendships of all the fellow near-death experiencers and researchers who have talked with me in interviews on my YouTube channel. I especially appreciate the support of Dr. Kenneth Ring, Dr. Jeffrey Long, Lisa Smartt, Dr. Raymond Moody, Rev. Peter Panagore, MDiv., Howard Storm, Daniel Giroux, Debra Diamond, Edward Salisbury, D.Div,F.D., Cherie Aimee, Jeffrey Olsen, Dr. Jeff O'Driscol, and Ines Byer. I am grateful for all the IANDS leaders and volunteers at the national and local conferences.

And, though it might sound strange to some people, I could not have completed this book without the love, guidance, and support from the other side. My father, Danny Barker; grandfather, Clyde Barker; and grandmother, Clara Barker, have been with me every step of the way, showing me that this book was supported by the heavens. I have had visits in spirit from my friend Clyde Boyd Jr. and my high school English teacher Mrs. Platzer who both whispered hints about loving scenes to include in this book. David Foster Wallace and Robin Williams appeared to me in lucid dreams, both letting me know on different occasions that they appreciate my focus on suicide prevention. I thank the many angels who comforted me as I wrote the difficult passages in this book and rejoiced with me as this project found its footing and walked out into the world.

ABOUT THE AUTHOR

As a college senior at The University of Texas at Austin, Tricia experienced an extraordinary near-death experience after a massive car wreck. In the afterlife, she learned that she must change her plans and work as a teacher. Tricia's near-death experience story has been featured on A&E's *I Survived: Beyond and Back* and covered by *National Geographic*. For over twenty years, Tricia has worked in schools and universities, often in impoverished areas. She helps others transform their lives in both the academic setting and in the spiritual community. Tricia's poetry and essays have been published in several publications including *The Binnacle*, *The Paterson Literary Review*, and *The Midwest Quarterly*. Currently, Tricia Barker is an English professor in Fort Worth, Texas. This is Tricia's first full-length book.